FLYING ON BROKEN *Wings*

FLYING ON BROKEN Wings

One woman's journey from poverty to prominence

PHYLLIS BIVINS-HUDSON, Ed.D.

Genceptz Consulting and Publishing
South Orange, New Jersey

FLYING ON BROKEN WINGS

This book is based on true events. The author has tried to recreate events, locales, and conversations from memory. To maintain anonymity, the author has changed the names of individuals and places. Some events have been slightly altered for entertainment, and some dialogue has been recreated.

Paperback ISBN-13: 978-0-578-74409-4

Published by Genceptz Consulting and Publishing
South Orange, NJ

Printed in the United States of America
First Edition September 2020

Cover Design by Make Your Mark Publishing Solutions
Interior Layout by Make Your Mark Publishing Solutions
Editing by Make Your Mark Publishing Solutions

DEDICATION

To my mother and father, who conceived me,
to my children, Tawana, Zammeah, and
Eric, who love me unconditionally,
to my granddaughters, Kamili, Kafi, Kai, and Nyla Lee,
and my sister, Annette,
to my husband, who rescued me
and to all my teachers, who invested in me,
this work is dedicated to you
My story …

FLYING ON BROKEN WINGS

I Was…
A beautiful golden baby!
Plumped up with rousing kisses, stolen smiles,
        Momma loving between the shadows
But envied secrets prevailed—
        in a moment sweltering of torn pain,
Clipped wings not yet ready to fly

Now I Have …
Fettered wings, young, and strong,
Bridled by bits of life's
winds,
        fate,
                evil,
Unable to break the momentum's grip
Struggling with a child's wisdom
        trying to
Fly on Broken Wings

I Have…
Unfettered notions
    poised and peppered along the lines of my life
Searching, finding me somewhere in between
    renovated hope,
        grit
            and freedom
        to
Fly on Broken Wings

        And
Now I Am…
Flying with all my stuff
    Against all odds, branding my savoir faire
    in that narrow space of found dreams
Resting in this season of lighted hope
        While
FLYING ON BROKEN WINGS

-Dr. Phyllis Geneva Bivins-Hudson

"The initial direction of our children's education will inevitably determine their future lives; however, those who defy the odds distinguish themselves among the masses."

-Dr. Phyllis Geneva Bivins-Hudson

INTRODUCTION

Geneva struggled to stop the streams of hot blood gushing down her face. She didn't know exactly where it was coming from, just that it was coming, and fast. She ran from it, frightened. Blood was everywhere, and it traveled with her as she cut through the wind, trying to rid herself of the mess.

What was she going to do? How could she hide it? What explanation would *she* be willing to accept? More importantly, what was her grandma going to do to her? The pain of old wounds haunted her as she anticipated her grandma's wrath. She somehow felt in touch with the stories she had been told about Jesus hanging from the cross.

The blood was still fresh, still streaming down her face, converging at her chin, its drops marching like toy soldiers onto her ragged burlap dress. Her vision was blurred, and the drops melted into each other, seeping into the dress like a plague devouring all in its path. She could hear her brother's faint voice in the near distance, but the words were like scrambled eggs. The pain was excruciating, throbbing, bringing with it more blood, then weakness in her knees. She'd been hurt badly. She thought she was going to die at a tender age.

Geneva thought about the origin of the pain. She thought even more about the consequences, knowing she would have some explaining to do, even though the whole thing was an accident. But there would be no immediate answers. Grandma Julia wouldn't care less about answers. She would come at Geneva full force with her rod of injustice, showing no compassion, no mercy. In fact, Grandma Julia's punishment could be far worse than any pain Geneva could imagine.

And it was.

When Grandma Julia learned that Geneva had been hit across the bridge of her nose with one of the large gunmetal bathing tubs, leaving a nasty gash, her hateful words of contempt were greater than the pain of the blow. She pierced a piece of Geneva's heart, corroding it with hate.

Blood did not excite Julia. The last words Geneva remembered from her grandma before blacking out were, "Ya shoulda bled ta death 'cause ya ain't had no biness messin' with dat tub." It never occurred to Grandma Julia that the accident was at the hands of someone else. To inflict further punishment, my dear mother, Geneva, wore that scar all her miserable life.

Julia had custody of two of her grandchildren, and she demonstrated, many times, that she favored the boy over the girl. That was life with my great-grandma Julia, who probably never knew how to love. A woman who had been a slave, if not by definition, certainly by her plight in the Rural South on the old homestead our family managed to own when it was almost unheard of for any black person to own property. That property consisted of a small piece of land and an old shanty.

My mother lost her mother when she was but a mere child of about eight years old. There were eight siblings, four girls and four boys, all no more than two years apart. Geneva and her brother Roshell were sent to live with Grandma Julia. According to my mother, her grandmother was a mean woman. She was downright abusive, mentally and physically.

When my mother began menstruating at fourteen years old, her grandmother, from ignorance, explained that having a period at fourteen was too young, and because she'd gotten it at such a young age, it was somehow brought upon her because she was being "too fast" and probably engaging in sexual activity. The consequence—a beating.

On another occasion, my mother and Roshell were playing, and he overexerted himself, triggering an asthma attack. My mother was blamed and beaten unmercifully as punishment. My uncle tried to explain and even bear the blame, but he was the favorite and never to be punished.

The beatings became a hallmark throughout my mother's adult life. The abuse followed her and found its way into every intimate relationship she had with men, except two: my sister's father, William Porter, affectionately known to me as Daddy Bill, and my biological father, Ernest Stevenson, neither of whom ever married her. Her violent relationships often caused her to do things to her own children that were inappropriate or abusive. My mother didn't always make the best decisions where I was concerned, some of which will be revealed in the pages to come. Many of her choices were correlated with her own abuse—both alcohol and physical abuse—which lasted until her untimely death from tuberculosis at the premature age of forty-seven years and six days.

I mention these abuses to elucidate reasons for some of what happened in my life. There is to be no mistake—despite what occurred between my mother and me, I loved her dearly. I felt sorry for the misery she suffered, and I hated all the abuse those men inflicted on her. This is not an attempt to tell her story. However, her mistakes helped direct my life down a different path. I purposely chose the road less traveled rather than follow the one on which I was being led. When I reached a life-changing intersection, I made a detour on the streets I'd paved for myself. I had to learn quickly and grow up even quicker. I experienced many things as a child that no child should ever endure. And I came to learn that when we seek to understand ourselves, we must not only consider those things from our childhood that shape us, but also those things from our parents' childhood as well.

Those of us who can't see the forest must make profound decisions to metacognitively comprehend that we cannot and *must* not be the apple that didn't fall too far from the tree. We must be solely responsible for picking ourselves up from the orchard and moving far enough away from the tree so we aren't left to rot. My hope was always to, one day, find at least one thread of joy that could be woven into the lyrics of my life.

As the great poet Maya Angelou stated in one of my favorite poems, in spite of life's circumstances, "Still I Rise."

CHAPTER 1

The Love Child

We lived in Disputanta for a short time, my mother and I. According to historic records, Disputanta was a remote, little unincorporated community in Prince George County, Virginia in the Richmond-Petersburg region, somewhere off U.S. Highway 460. The town's origin is a part of several neighboring towns: Waverly, Wakefield, Ivor, and Windsor, which was my mom's birthplace. The town was made up of relatively modest two-story homes, mostly owned by whites, who also owned most of the surrounding properties and those in the vicinity. Many of them lived off the land but also used produce from their crops to earn a living. People like my mother worked those fields for the white landowners.

Mom said we lived in Disputanta because she'd found work as a field hand and room and board. My mother had only a sixth-grade education, having left school at eleven or twelve to work, so work for her was often fieldwork or house cleaning or whatever she could get to earn an honest living. She was nineteen and lived with a white Disputanta family, working in their fields from sunup to sundown. In exchange, they gave her free room and board. She chopped the weeds away from the vegetables, picked cucumbers, peanuts, cotton, beans, and whatever else was necessary. She also cleaned their house and helped with other odd jobs that needed attending.

Mom was married to Jack Bivins, but their marriage was not more than an intermittent relationship, because the prison system became a revolving door for him. While married to Jack, she was also being pursued by another gentleman caller named Ernest Stevenson. They dated off and on during Jack's frequent prison stints. Ernest was a long-distance truck driver, and he eventually became my biological father, although Jack was always of the notion that he had fathered me. According to Mom, Ernest often stopped by to see her while in route to one of his destinations. He never visited without bringing niceties. On at least one occasion, he even brought her a T-bone steak. He began calling her "T-bone" because of the way she devoured that steak, leaving only the bone. Knowing she had little or no social life, he took her for long rides in his rig, sometimes in the middle of the night while everyone else was asleep. He'd bring her back in enough time to get a couple of hours of sleep before rising early for the fields. Eventually, one of those late-night rendezvouses led to my conception—their love child.

Another field worker was sweet on Ernest, too, so she and Mom were rivals. When Ernest snuck by at night to visit, Viola always made sure she was available, inching her way into every conversation and involving herself in every situation. Viola even freshened up when she thought Ernest would show. Mom grew tired of the competition and decided to take action. She confronted Viola and demanded that she stay away from Ernest. The ladies argued fiercely, and Ernest had a time trying to bring them under control while keeping the white folks in the house from learning what was going on. If they found out about the bickering, it could cost one or both their jobs, not to mention the punishment that would beset Ernest since he was in "good ol' boys" territory. He tried to be nice to them both. When he brought Mom something special, he also brought something for Viola; albeit, Viola's tokens weren't as personal as Mom's. Ernest didn't know how to put Viola down easily for fear of hurting her feelings, so his niceness was mistaken for affection.

Finally, Viola realized her attempts were futile, and she gave up ... or so it seemed. On one unusually hot and humid day, the field hands thirsted for a breeze and a cool drink of water to help temper the thick air. Periodically, they stopped chopping weeds, turning soil, or picking cotton to straighten their backs, wipe the briny sweat from their faces in the hemline of their dresses, and inhale the heat of the day. So when Viola abruptly left her fieldwork and proceeded to the main house, no one paid attention to the sudden movement. It wasn't unusual for a worker to leave the field and return to the main house to use the outhouse or get a cool drink of water from the well if they ran out of the water the lady of the house had prepared for them.

A loud scream could be heard from the main house to the fields. Everyone looked up, but Geneva not only looked up, she looked on in horror and dropped her hoe, recognizing the scream—her baby. Frantic, she sprinted through the fields, leaping through the rows of freshly plowed ground like an African cheetah. Her face was pale, and her mouth was a powder house. Big beads of sweat charged down her face. Her legs were rubber, weakening from swift movements over uneven ground. The frightful screams continued to drum in her ears, charging her forward, providing the energy she needed to make the trek. The screams grew louder the closer she got to the house, a life-threatening crescendo.

At last, when she reached the main house, she bolted through the back door and found her baby girl, too young yet to walk. Viola was holding me down on the eye of a large fully lit cast iron cook stove. The lady of the house, Miss Ann, had built a fire to begin cooking lunch for the field hands. Viola saw me crawling around in the kitchen while Miss Ann was in another room and decided she'd get even with Geneva by putting her baby on the heated stove.

Geneva, in a fit of anger and fear, struck Viola, knocking her away from the stove and onto the floor. She quickly scooped me into her arms and saw that my little bottom was raw like a fresh piece of uncooked meat. The tender layer of skin was still on the eye of the stove, and the room smelled of burning flesh.

I screamed uncontrollably. Mom was in a panic. She didn't know what to do. For a few seconds, she paced in deep thought. Disputanta was a remote area. There were no hospitals around and only one doctor that she knew of. He was miles away and, to her knowledge, he didn't treat colored folks. But she was desperate. She set out running in the blazing sun, wearing her field clothes, with a rag tightly wrapped around her head. She held me with one hand under my back and the other under my bottom, careful not to touch the affected area.

The ninety-degree weather tired her out quickly, but she never stopped running until she reached the town area of Disputanta. The town had several stores that carried supplies for almost all its residents' needs, from food to farm equipment. There were banks and an ice cream and soda shop, a business building, and other small establishments. Inside the business building was the doctor's office.

My mother never stopped to consider the elevator. She never stopped to realize she was colored and had no right to be where she was. She ran up five flights of stairs and burst into the doctor's office, past the receptionist unannounced. The doctor, who was seeing another patient, insisted she leave. But she was determined.

"Doctor, please take a look at my child. She's been burned!" she pleaded as I continued to scream.

The doctor refused and showed her the door, but she resisted, remaining steadfast.

"If you don't leave right now, I'll have to call the sheriff," he warned.

Desperate, Mom turned me over on my stomach and laid me on the patient's lap. The white woman screamed at the gruesome sight.

The doctor didn't respond right away but, finally, he said to the patient, "Do you mind if I treat this gal's child first?"

The woman, happy to have the little black half-baked baby away from her, blurted, "No, go right ahead. I can wait."

So the doctor treated my raw buttocks. "Now, how are you going to pay this bill?" he asked.

"I don't know yet. I work for Miss Ann, and she don't gimme much money 'cause I stay wit' her, and I eat free. But I can give you most of what I get till the bill is paid, if that's all right, sir."

"I guess that'll be fine. I know Ann, and I'll be checking by there from time to time. When I stop by, you can pay me whatever you have then. How did you get to town, anyway?"

"I run all the way."

"You ran damn near five miles to get here, gal?"

"Yessir. My baby was in trouble."

When she left, she decided to take the elevator down, finally feeling the pain in her legs from working all day and running almost five miles. She felt deathly ill from exhaustion and an empty stomach.

The white lady from the doctor's office boarded the elevator with her. "Girl, you want a ride back to Ann's house?"

"Yes, ma'am."

"I'll take you. I live down the road from Ann. Here, the doctor asked me to see to it that you get this bill and this bag of stuff, too, for your baby."

"He gave me a bill already."

"Well, he said to give you this one, too." She handed her another folded note. "Open it up. Can you read, girl?"

"Yes'm, I can read."

My mother read the note. Somehow, the bill was paid in full.

She never confirmed how the bill was taken care of, but she had an idea, since the white lady was so anxious for her to open it. As for Viola, she was seen scrambling to gather all her things before my mother arrived. I guess she knew what to expect upon her return.

CHAPTER 2

Improvising: Products of Small Miracles

Poor black folks wrote the book on improvising. When I was growing up, we didn't have a lot, but we were rich in some things and poor in others. We often made do by extemporizing. In fact, my first recollection of literacy was when my mom taught me the alphabet. I remember the excitement of watching her rip off the flap of a cardboard box and print the letters as neatly as she could onto the flap with black liquid Esquire shoe polish. Some of the letters would drip and run, but they were adequate for me to understand and learn to recite and write them. Our box flap and shoe polish were the equivalent of the more sophisticated flashcards and markers.

This was a high time for me. Learning gave me great joy. I still remember the letters, but none were more impressive than the "A" because the black polish on the right side of the letter would dramatically drip off the cardboard. I loved looking at it flow gracefully across the ridges of the box flap and down onto the newspaper that caught it on the floor. Even today, when I write my A's, I always drag the right leg, looping it around the bottom to make sure it doesn't drip off the page. But every letter mattered. It made me feel important knowing that, soon, I would be able to combine those letters and form words, so when the grownups spelled words they didn't want children to recognize, I would know their secrets.

Once I learned the alphabet, I was unstoppable. I picked up each sound effortlessly, and before I entered kindergarten, Mom said I was reading more words than even my cousins, who were attending school already. School would become my refuge and my fortress, and reading had already garnered a permanent place in my heart. While I was not yet old enough to be enrolled in school, I wanted to be there. I was anxious about it. I wanted to learn and read all the books with the stories I remembered my mother telling me about. I wanted to see the pictures of Little Sally Walker and Goldie Locks. I could envision them and wanted to be closer to them, to be a part of the experience. But the children I knew all began school at the magical age of six. For me, that was another source of anxiety because I didn't turn six until December of 1959, which meant I'd missed the September cutoff and would not be able to start school until September of the following year, making me almost seven years old. This prompted me to start my own utopic school with imaginary students. Mom said I read everything. And since we had only one book in the house, that meant reading food labels, words on buildings, words on appliances, cars, billboards, and anything else that had letters. Mom said I practiced a lot, attempting to read words even she didn't know how to pronounce.

There were other challenges, too, like having adequate clothing or shoes to wear. In fact, owning a pair of new shoes was a small miracle. Even more miraculous was how long they lasted. When the bottom wore out, Mom would take a piece of cardboard from a box and trace a narrow outline of my foot for a perfect fit. Then she placed the cardboard inside the shoes to cover the holes that had worn into the bottoms. The quick fix usually lasted a while, until it rained or snowed; then Mom would remove the cardboard until it dried overnight and put it back the next day, unless it was too badly damaged, which meant constructing a new pattern if there was cardboard material around. When there was no cardboard, layers of discarded newspaper or brown paper bags would substitute.

I never complained. In fact, a "new" pair of shoes was not new at all. They were usually leftover shoes Mom had managed to scrape up enough money to purchase from the shoe repair shop in Downtown Suffolk on Main Street because no one bothered to pick them up. I always believed those shoes were left there as one of God's ways of making provisions for me. I hated to part with my shoes, so I was glad when Mom extended their life. There was one problem with them, however—none of them ever fit properly. I had what Mom called "king feet," her way of describing my wide feet. I needed an extra wide width shoe because none of those "new" shoes were accommodating. But it didn't matter because, no matter what shoes we had, my size or not, Mom would tug, push, and hit the bottoms repeatedly to get them on my feet. The task was often accompanied by beads of sweat racing down her forehead. It was hard work, but I helped her as much as possible. I'd push my foot in as best I could. I'd even curl my toes so the shoe would appear to fit.

When they were finally on, Mom would say, "Stand up, puddin', and lemme see how they fit."

They were sometimes so tight that when I attempted to stand, I immediately fell back onto the chair. The shock of the pain disoriented me, but I didn't dare complain because I'd have no shoes, and Mom would be furious with me for being ungrateful. She'd say, "You tryin' to be cute. Well, it ain't no time to be cute, 'cause if you can't wear these here shoes, yo' black ass gonna be barefooted this winter."

I knew she was angry when she used the a-word, and I also knew it was best to get those shoes on at any cost and act like they didn't hurt. After all, I needed those shoes for school. Nothing was going to stop me from an opportunity to read and write and hear those stories I had grown to love so much.

One time, I had a second pair of shoes, which became my Sunday shoes. I had received them from a neighbor whose child had outgrown them. She watched in disbelief as Mom and I struggled through the shoe ritual, trying to get my king feet into queen shoes that seemed to be two sizes too small for me.

She said, "Geneva, you sure she can wear them shoes?"

"Yeah, she can wear them. She just got king feet, but she'll grow into them."

I certainly didn't need to grow into them. I had already grown *out* of them. But once we got home, Mom reminded me that I should reserve that pair for Sundays. I was just glad Sunday only came four times a month. Mom knew they didn't fit properly because she cut the pinky toe out of them to give me a little more room and replaced the toe opening with a piece of cardboard that she'd polished black with Esquire shoe polish, so the neighbor wouldn't think we weren't thankful for the shoes. On Sundays when I wore them, the top and sides of my pinky toes were black from the shoe polish, and the bottoms were sometimes black because they'd drag along on the ground, picking up all the dirt from exposure to the elements. When I finally got a new pair of shoes years later, they were purchased from the Bootery Shop in Uptown Suffolk on E. Washington Street, near the Suffolk Lunch Room, a popular eatery, where many Suffolkians met and ate.

At six years old, I often went without other necessities. I don't remember my first pair of panties but, again, we improvised. One day, after playing outside, I paraded down Duke Street with a bunch of kids, headed for home. I was the last stop at what was called the Big House, the last house on the right side of the street, where Mom and I lived temporarily. It was Miss Sadie's juke joint. The sanctified church ladies said it was a house of ill repute.

We played and talked, doing all the things little kids did. Then it happened. In my frolicking, I'd forgotten my mother's warning and jumped one time too many. My panties fell to the ground. They belonged to Mom. An enormous safety pin in the side kept them up, but all the jumping around caused the panties to loosen, and they dropped past my knees without warning. I quickly stepped out of them and kept going, as if I didn't know what happened or to whom they belonged.

As luck would have it, Miss Sadie's dog, Briscoe, who was my favorite friend, had come to meet me. He immediately began barking, and he picked up the panties with his mouth. I tried to get him to release them, but he wouldn't. "Briscoe, put them down. Leave 'em alone, Briscoe. Move. Go on home," I said quietly. But Briscoe knew I had dropped something, and he wanted to help.

Finally, the kids saw Briscoe and me, and they figured out right away what happened. They began laughing, taunting, and teasing, as kids do.

"Ah ha! You dropped your drawers."

"Phyllis, yo' mama bloomers fell off. You better get 'em fo' you go home without 'em and get a beatin'."

I left them there, still pretending they weren't mine. I ran home, fearing someone would pull my dress up and discover my lie. I bounced inside the house as if nothing happened. Mom never suspected anything, and Briscoe kept my secret. However, I later learned that one of the kids told her mother about the incident, and she, in turn, told my mother. When Mom approached me about it, I told her the truth, but I knew buying me a pair of panties was not a priority; we had other pressing issues, like where our next meal would come from or if we could remain in our living quarters for another week.

Mom found temporary work from a white lady in town for whom she worked a few days a month. The woman had a son about two years younger than me, and she was getting rid of some of his clothes. "Geneva, I know you have a child. Maybe you can use some of my son's shorts and shirts that he's outgrown," she said.

Mom thanked her and gladly accepted the things, excited about bringing them home to sift through and see if there was anything we could use. She arrived home and told me she had a nice surprise for me. When I opened the bag and saw those shorts and shirts, I was overjoyed. I was growing like a weed and desperately needed some "new" clothes. I tried them all on. Each pair of shorts were a skin-tight fit. But even skin tight was better than what I had. I was tall and skinny, with a round butt and big legs, making it difficult to fit comfortably into many of the items.

While rummaging through the bag of clothes, I came upon the steal of the century—swimming trunks with a pair of briefs attached inside. I yelled, "Ma, look!"

"What is it?" she said.

"Look what I found."

Together, we gingerly tore the underpants away from the trunks. When done, I held them up, stretching them to capacity. "Ta-da! I got me a pair of panties. My own panties. Yeah!"

I finally had some underpants that almost fit. They were white and extremely tight, but they were mine. I didn't even mind the front fly opening; it was a minor inconvenience. Mom saw it as a reason to remind me to sit like a lady because, "If you don't, when you move the wrong way, the hole will open and anybody will be able to see everything God gave you."

Those panties lasted me a long time, too. I wore them until the thick, reinforced leg band began to split up the side. I wore them every day. My mother taught me how to take them off at night, wash them, and hang them neatly on the back of one of the wooden kitchen chairs we owned, so they would be dry, clean, and ready for the next morning.

CHAPTER 3

Embarrassing Moments

Wearing and losing Mom's panties wasn't the only embarrassing episode I experienced as a six-year-old. I used to have two sun-kissed plaits that rested on my shoulders. They were mouse brown in the winter and a muted strawberry blonde in the summer. My bangs were layers of small crinkled curls, lying obediently in a pile, thanks to the water and Royal Crown hair dressing that activated my natural curls. My hair never remained straight no matter how much it was combed or brushed. It was like my daddy's natural curly hair. But my caretakers in my mother's absence thought my hair should be more like the other children's hair. Theirs had to be straightened with a hot comb. Mine didn't need extreme heat, but the elder ladies sat me down in one of those heavy chrome kitchen chairs with thick cushioned seats and began heating that straightening comb to fry my hair.

Depending on who was dressing my hair that day, she'd place a comb on an old wood-burning stove, or the open flame of a gas stove, or the more sophisticated hot comb heater until the straightening comb was hot. Then the comb was wiped on a piece of cloth as part of the cooling process, ensuring that it wasn't too hot for my hair. I was reminded to hold my ear downward to prevent the comb from accidentally burning it. However, avoiding the ear often meant burning my fingers. The hot comb was pulled through sectioned pieces of my hair repeatedly until it was bone straight. The worst part of the experience was when it came time to straighten the edges, which required the hair dresser to come dangerously close—sometimes too close—to the temple and sides as well as the nape. Usually, I received a warning not to move, or I would be burned. But more often than not, it didn't matter because even the most skilled beautician sometimes burned my hair and skin. When done, my scalp was red and charred.

The finished coiffure resulted in nothing more than my hair falling closely to my head, reluctantly settling into an unrehearsed heap. Small clumps of hair that couldn't tolerate the fierce heat left empty spaces on my head. Excessive straightening eventually resulted in a head full of half-dollar-sized scabs and sores filled with puss and blood. My mother tried her best to correct the problem by picking the remaining hair from the sores, hoping to remove the scabs, clean up the matted fur, and free the hair. But her plan failed. One empty space left a bald spot about the size of a quarter on the back center of my head. I tried to cover up that patchy bald spot by combing hair over it, but to no avail. For years, that spot would be a source of embarrassment and ridicule from my peers.

Mom was advised to take me to a doctor. Of course, there were no black dermatologists in our small town. But there was Dr. Weinberger, on North Main Street in Downtown Suffolk, who knew nothing about black people's hair or how to care for it. I don't even know if he was a dermatologist. His only remedy: "We have to shave her head."

Believing that to be the only option, Mom concurred. So right there in Dr. Weinberger's office, I left my glory in a heap on the floor. I cried. For a girl during the 50s and 60s, being bald was not fashionable. Eventually, my hair grew back, but as it came in, so did an extreme case of eczema. We returned to Dr. Weinberger, and he shared the diagnosis with Mom but failed to treat it. Instead, he did what he did best—grabbed his clippers and shaved my hair off again, as if I were his son, there for my weekly haircut. I was bald a second time and, again, the source of amusement for my peers. Even today, I am reminded of the condition. I never received treatment, and, as a result, the hair follicles around the edges began to thin and eventually all died, leaving no chance for new hair growth. C'est la vie.

CHAPTER 4

The Big House

Dreadful anomalies seemed to follow me, and the Big House, being everything the church ladies had spoken of, was the source of much of that dread. The children often played hide 'n' seek. All the rooms upstairs and downstairs provided plenty of wonderful hiding places. But some of the adults somehow forgot how to play the game. Mr. Fetch was one of those adults. He didn't play fairly nor did he care to know the rules; he made his own. In fact, he wasn't even invited to play with us.

Mr. Fetch lived in the Big House, too. He was Miss Sadie's live-in boyfriend, and since he was usually there to watch us, we had permission to play in the Big House. After romping up and down the stairs for what seemed like hours, going from one room to the next lined up like a human train and holding each other by the shoulders, we grew tired and began playing hide 'n' seek. We all took turns hiding and finding each other. Suddenly, something strange happened. I didn't hear the others anymore.

Mr. Fetch was in the next room waiting for me as I attempted to pass through in search of the other children. I was only six years old and thought it was strange for him to want to play with only me, but it seemed he had decided to do just that.

"Where is everyone?" I asked.

"I sent them all downstairs to play," he said.

I wanted to go downstairs, too, and wondered why I had been chosen to stay upstairs. He patted the spot next to him on the bed as he whispered, "Be quiet and come sit next to me."

I didn't know why, but my heart sensed something was wrong, and it began racing until it hurt. What he was asking of me didn't feel right. I was reluctant to move. He grabbed my scrawny waist and pulled me over to him. My heart hurt even more. It was beating too fast, and I couldn't control it. I wished my mother was there with me to make him stop. Tears began to well up in my eyes. I was frightened because Mr. Fetch was a scary-looking man. His face was repulsive, with sagging skin and sunken, low-hanging jowls. He had powdery mouse-gray, scaly skin with large warts all over his dried-out face, neck, and arms, and his eyes were bloodshot. Mr. Fetch was very skinny, about 5'10", and hosted only two or three teeth in his mouth. He smoked cigarettes and had a deep, nasty cough that made his body heave whenever the coughing spells began. The grown folks used to say he had "consumption." Most children were afraid of him, but because he was Miss Sadie's man, we all had to talk to him. We accepted him because we were accustomed to him, but under the circumstances, the ugliness of his behavior made his unpleasant face more unbearable.

I didn't try very hard to resist him because he said if I did, I would force him to hurt me. I had seen men hurt my mother before and how it made her cry, so I began to cry on the inside, afraid that if I gave myself permission to cry aloud, he'd beat me or punch me. But the tears rebelled and would not behave themselves. They fought with me and eventually won, sliding silently from the corners of my eyes.

"Shh. Just relax and lay back on the bed," he said in a jagged voice.

He tugged on my panties and managed to pull them down around my ankles. I was terrified and frozen. I lay there, with my tears telling me to do something, but I didn't know what to do. The tip of my index finger hooked my bottom lip, pulling it down as I stared at the ceiling.

His spikey voice whispered to me again, but I don't remember what he said because my little six-year-old mind tried to block out what was happening to me. He moved away from my ear and looked down at my vagina, watching his finger as he guided it to the little opening. He tried to force it inside me, but I couldn't keep still because it hurt so badly. I wiggled constantly from the pain as he whispered in my ear to keep quiet.

He kissed my ear and tried to get on top of me. But the other children ran back upstairs and into the room just in time to see him pushing me away and scolding me in a stern voice. "Put your panties back on," he said, as if I'd been trying to seduce him.

All the children were older than me, so they knew more about what was going on than I did. I wanted badly for them to tell because I couldn't. Mr. Fetch made it clear that if I told, something bad would happen to me. But he never said *they* couldn't tell. Yet, no one spoke for me, and Mr. Fetch went free as I suffered in silence.

From that day, I never allowed myself to be in his company alone, although he'd tried on several other occasions to lure me into his secret space. I fought back as best I could for a six-year-old. I stayed away, and even when others questioned why I seemed to be uncomfortable in his presence, I never told them about the dirty little secret. Years later, I recognized him in an old photo with my stepfather and my little sister. She was around eight or so. I wondered if he had invited her into his forbidden lair. I wondered if any of the other children had shared an unspoken secret about Mr. Fetch.

Being an added addition to the Big House made me an easy target for Mr. Fetch because he had full access. Mom had a sleep-in job in New York City, which was a fancy phrase for a black woman living in the maid's quarters of a white family's home, working as a housekeeper, cooking, cleaning, and caring for their children. There was no work to speak of in the three-square-mile town of Suffolk, so she'd gone north for a so-called better life for her and me. Her absences were always difficult for me, this one especially because, while Mom was away, I wasn't watched as closely as I should have been. Sure, I was well fed, I had clothes on my back and a place to sleep, but no one was there when Mr. Fetch wanted to play hide 'n' seek.

The Big House lived up to its heathenistic reputation. Friday through Sunday, the house took on a persona all her own. There was always something we children found exciting. Once the Friday sun went down, the strong smell of collard greens, fried fish, and fried chicken danced through the rooms, tickling our noses, making pit stops at each nostril. Ole Dad, as everyone called him, sat in his usual spot near the front door in the old straight-back rocking chair that seemed to groan every time he moved methodically back and forth. He was more than ninety years old, blind but didn't wear any dark glasses, so we stayed away from him because we were afraid of the yellowish-green puss that kept his eyes permanently shut. He kept a homemade cane near him, and he constantly tapped it on the floor. He knew the name of anyone entering the Big House because of the sound of their voices and footsteps. He engaged in conversations with all of them as they swarmed the Big House for the weekend party that would leave folks with their "heads bad," which meant they were drunk from too much corn liquor.

Ole Dad was on the first floor. The children had free reign of the house, so we went back and forth from upstairs to downstairs, zipping past him. We found fun in trying to make him guess which of us had just passed. He always seemed to know. We spent a great deal of our time downstairs where Ole Dad was, in part, because that's where the piccolo was, a misnomer for the jukebox.

The crowd downstairs fed the piccolo and danced until they wore themselves out doing the boogie woogie, the swing, the jitterbug, the jive, and the twist. But as kids, we were never tired. In fact, I was an excellent dancer, and the grown folks often pit me against other children to compete for quarters. It was one of the few things I could win. I won often and nearly always walked away with twenty-five or fifty cents and on a good night, maybe even a dollar or two. I could do all the popular dances. Some of the other children would get angry because, no matter how hard they danced, I was a formidable opponent who simply loved what she did.

Upstairs was a different atmosphere. On one occasion, in one of the gambling rooms where the children weren't supposed to be, the whole table was engaged in a serious game of bid whist. Miss Lula Belle and Mr. Char Lee were a couple, who, together, had nineteen children. They were always at the Big House on Friday and Saturday nights, trying to win some extra money to help feed their army. This Saturday night was going well for them. They had bet several times and won big. Miss Lula Belle decided to step out on her own and bet all they had on the last hand of the evening. They lost that hand, and Mr. Char Lee became so enraged that he leapt over the table and yanked Miss Lula Belle's hair, relieving her of her wig. She screamed and struggled to cover her head because most people had never seen her hair before. It was a matted mess. She had a perfectly shaped football head that was almost bald. There was a small plait on each corner of her head and a larger one dead center. Big brown scabs of what looked like psoriasis filled in the other areas. On hot summer days, Miss Lula Belle could be seen on her porch from afar picking those scabs. She used to tell us children that picking her scabs was how she kept her nerves calm. And I was one of the little ones selected to comb and scratch her nasty scabs, since I ate at her house regularly.

We stood outside the door, peeking and laughing raucously at the sight of Miss Lula Belle's half-bald head. But she soon recovered, and it was on! She jumped up from the table, and the two of them began fighting. They fought all over the upstairs area then fell partially down the stairs together on top of each other. They got up and continued fighting until Miss Sadie signaled the bouncer to open the door. She gave them both a swift shove, and out the door they went, onto the street where the fighting continued. They lived across the street and fought all the way home. We watched until we couldn't see them anymore. Meanwhile, the games continued, and we went back inside because, after all, this was Saturday night, and we didn't want to miss the next show—whatever it might be.

Another time, while several of the men were shooting craps, Mr. Cauty Mer was accused of cheating. Mr. Cleve, his accuser, got mad and wanted to fight. Miss Sadie got in the middle of the melee and made the mistake of turning her back on Mr. Cleve as he attempted to stab Mr. Cauty Mer. He plunged the knife into Miss Sadie's back, just over her right shoulder, which would've been near Mr. Cauty Mer's heart. We all stood silent and amazed, waiting to see what would happen next because we knew Miss Sadie didn't take no stuff from nobody. We'd even seen her fight policemen. I'd also seen her fight off the dogs the policemen put on people during civil rights battles. I had witnessed plenty as a six-year-old—fighting, womanizing, my mom's abuse—but never a stabbing.

That night, Miss Sadie didn't have to do anything to Mr. Cleve because one of her ten children, George Michael, was there. He had an awful temper. Someone ran downstairs to where he was bumping and grinding on the dance floor with Sweetie Mae to "Your Precious Love," by Jerry Butler, which he shouldn't have been doing because he was supposed to be my mama's man. George Michael pushed Sweetie Mae away from him like she smelled funny or something and ran up the stairs quicker than a jackrabbit. He asked no questions as he commenced to beating and punching on Mr. Cleve until Mr. Cleve was down on the floor helpless. George Michael straddled him and kept punching his face and head until Mr. Cleve finally gave up the ghost. No one attempted to stop George Michael, not even his mother. We didn't know it then, but we wouldn't see him for a long time after that because Mr. Cleve died, and George Michael had to go to the Virginia Department of Corrections in Culpeper County, where he spent many years for killing Mr. Cleve.

There were other interesting spots in the Big House. Downstairs in the middle of the dance floor was a large burlap rug. But underneath that area rug was a large rectangular part of the floor that had been cut out. To get it open, Mr. Fetch used his pocketknife to lift the edge of the door, exposing the ground underneath the house. Many of the houses stood off the ground on brick pillars about two feet high. This was where they kept the extra corn liquor. Selling it was illegal, so they had to keep it out of sight. On at least one occasion, a county policeman had come to raid the Big House. When he knocked on the door loudly with his baton, everybody inside recognized the knock, even me. I was closest to the floor opening, where I had been cutting a rug, but I intuitively stepped aside so the real rug could be swiftly moved. Mr. Fetch opened the floor-door quickly with his pocketknife and pushed me down in the hole, jamming a gallon jug of corn liquor into my little hands. Once I was down there, the door closed, and they replaced the rug.

I was scared in that small, dark hole but didn't say a word because I knew enough about these kinds of raids from other times when policemen had broken down the front door, arresting everyone for selling illegal moonshine. The police officer was allowed in, and he asked why it had taken so long to open the door. Miss Sadie knew the officer well; we all did. To the adults, he was "Big Foot," but to us children, he was "Mr. Big Foot" because he had enormous feet, and he was exceptionally tall, with a huge frame. Miss Sadie apologized and said we couldn't hear him because of the music coming from the piccolo. He must've been suspicious because he searched the premises without a search warrant. I could hear and feel him walking over my head. In fact, he stopped right over the floor-door. Then he moved, and the sound of his footsteps became faint. He wandered upstairs and did what he always did whenever he saw men illegally shooting craps in the Big House or on the porch of any of the abandoned houses in Pond Town—took all the money he saw. After all, it was illegal gambling.

He finally left, and I was released from that dark hole, where I'd been for what seemed like a short eternity. I was still frightened, but no one cared as long as the precious commodity was protected. Losing it would've meant a loss of money, and money was too hard to come by to lose frivolously.

CHAPTER 5

From Pond Town to Hoboken and Back

One of the best memories I have of the Big House happened one Saturday night. The house was jumping. Every room was filled with gambling, singing, dancing, drinking, eating, and arguing. Suddenly, there was another familiar knock on the door. It got my attention as I stood waiting for someone to open it. I knew who it was, but we were told to never open the door, for fear of strangers or Mr. Big Foot. Eventually, someone opened it, and there stood the most beautiful woman I'd ever seen in my life. It was my mom! She had taken a bus from New York City and come home to me. Her baby soft pecan brown face was topped by tiny, too-tight, shiny black curls. She wore candy apple red lipstick and an orange and brown soft wool plaid pencil skirt. Her round clip-on earbobs were accented by faux mink centers, and a faux mink stole was draped over her shoulders. She looked like a movie star. I was overjoyed to see her. She had come back for me! I beamed with excitement and made more money dancing that night than I had ever made. But I was really dancing for my mom. I danced hard and long, then fell fast asleep in her arms. She was all mine.

Her visit wouldn't last long, though. Mom had to return to work in New York. But this time, I went with her most of the way. It was time for me to be enrolled in school, and I couldn't attend kindergarten in Suffolk because Mom removed me from the Big House. I don't know if she suspected I had been molested or if she didn't have enough money to pay for my stay, but I left. Off we went, with a stop-over on Park Street in Hoboken, New Jersey, where I would begin kindergarten while living with Uncle Roshell, Aunt Margie, Hortense, and baby Keith.

Except for Aunt Mary and Aunt Gladys Lee, all Mom's siblings occupied one floor of the Hoboken apartment building on Park Street. This was another time of mirth for me. There was Uncle Ben, Uncle Roshell, Uncle June, and Uncle WT, with their wives or significant others and all my cousins. What a great moment in my life. I was enrolled into school, and Mom returned to New York to her job.

Kindergarten was an exciting experience. I couldn't wait to show off my writing skills with my fanciful letter A and my ability to decipher and spell words and read some of those books that I would later learn had been reserved for first graders. I sat at a large, round table with a big K for kindergarten on it. My cousin Hortense was in first grade, and she was in the same room; however, her class was on the other side of the room, with tables labeled with a 1 for first grade. I insisted on being at the first-grade table and cried until I got my way. The work must have been easy because I wasn't moved back to the K table. After all, I was already reading. I remained in Hoboken until first grade. The sleep-in job ended, and Mom picked me up. We returned to Suffolk to start all over again.

I started first grade at Mary Estes Elementary School in Pond

Town. School began September 1960, and I was six years and nine months old. I turned seven in December. I met my first-grade teacher, Miss Jones. Although she was nice to me, I was frightened of her because a large, fleshy black mole sat on the crease between her nose and cheek. The older kids said it was a huge booger and I didn't want it to get on me. Miss Jones tried to hug me because I was inconsolable when my mother left me. She knew I was experiencing separation anxiety, but I was too young to understand her intent. I couldn't get past the mole. It was the source of my first unpleasant school experience. However, somehow, I adjusted because I remained in Miss Jones's class for the entire school year.

Like the Big House, Pond Town was a popping place, too. It had not just one big house but a series of houses where corn liquor, state liquor, and beer were sold as a way of living, along with the usual Friday and Saturday night fish fries, rent parties, and fist fights. Summer Friday and Saturday nights were the best because school was out and us children partook in all that Pond Town had to offer, even though much of what went on should not have been available to us. The most prominent of the big houses in Pond Town was run by Miss Annie Bland, who was short in stature and known for her elaborate rhinestone-rimmed cat-eye glasses, full front row of gleaming gold teeth, and fancy clothes. Her adult daughter, Billie Rae, had a little girl's voice, always speaking like she was still in puberty, looking to minimize the power she actually had over the men who frequented their "place of business." She was every man's dream. Men would frequent Miss Annie Bland's house just to get a look at Billie Rae. And us girls always saw her as someone to emulate when we grew up because she had a fierce body, beautiful cocoa brown skin, a pretty face, and a charm that seemed to captivate everyone. We didn't learn until years later that Miss Annie Bland and her daughter, Billie Rae, were selling much more than corn liquor.

When we were older, we understood why our parents forbade us to go to "The House of Annie Bland."

As much fun as we were having, our move back to Pond Town was short lived but would be reoccurring.

Not many things excited me as much as a good meal and being in school, learning new things. It was time to return to school as a second grader. An exhilarating feeling always came over me at the mention of school. It was my private sanctuary, where I could go and feel like somebody. It took me to a place that got me high off the stories I read and the places those stories took me. School provided a temporary escape from my world of poverty. I was a bright child and soaked up the knowledge, and my intellect swelled with every morsel of information my teachers gave me. So I was ready for grade two, although I had to attend at three different locations during a ten-month span because I kept moving around. In fact, by the time I enrolled into second grade, I had been homeless about seven times. But the next three moves during second grade would each come with a price to pay. I was enrolled into Ida Easter Elementary School in Saratoga, another sub-division of Suffolk, where I met my teacher, Miss Gray. I was small with big legs, and people constantly made negative comments about how puny I was, with "white girl" legs.

I was born in Saratoga, on Ashley Avenue, and was living in Saratoga again with Mom and her husband, Jack, whom I thought was my biological father. He was home temporarily. He'd spent most of his adult life in prison. We lived in a large house in Saratoga with Jack's mom, MinyNar Jordan, and her husband, Mr. Eel, who wasn't the father of MinyNar's ten adult children. Although they were all adults, any number of her other children moved in and out of the house whenever they needed a place to stay when they were between jobs. Even though MinyNar and Mr. Eel had a full house, like many southern households living with extended family, there was always room for one more—in this case, Mom and me. Living there had its privileges. I was fed and had a place to sleep and clothes to wear. I attended church regularly. But most importantly, I was able to go to my sanctuary, school.

MinyNar was the matriarch. If she said it, it became law. We did exactly as she said, or we'd have to "pick up our things and move on." She ran a strict household, and any wrongdoing was subject to her wrath. She didn't have an outside job, but she took care of her household. And anyone living there of working age was expected to contribute in some way to the upkeep of the house. If any of the adults ran short on cash during the week, she always seemed to have a little extra. But if they didn't work, they had to go to school. Tony (who I thought was one of my first cousins) and I went to school, which was fine by me because school was my favorite place to be. And I was starting a new school, so that meant learning new and more challenging information.

MinyNar was a religious zealot, and she practiced "holiness," which meant being a sanctified Pentecostal Christian. In her house, that also meant everybody was required to practice being holy, at least on Sundays. We spent the entire Sabbath at church. The only person to whom this rule didn't apply was Mr. Eel, who never went to church, but he didn't work on Sundays. Tony and I were the same age, and we went to church every Sunday, rain or shine, along with MinyNar and anyone who had slept in that house on Saturday night. We were there for Sunday school, morning worship, lunch, afternoon service, dinner, and the evening service. As children, with nothing else to do with our Sunday time, Tony and I enjoyed the experience. We especially loved the part when everyone got to eat, and we looked forward to a visit from the Holy Ghost because that meant watching the parishioners dance and roll around on the floor in the Spirit. We mocked MinyNar when she got the Holy Ghost, jumping up and down, shouting. She was a big, burly woman, and when she leapt from her seat, the floorboards jumped with her. Her shouts created a rhythm with the subtle squeaks and other sounds from the floor. Every jump brought out a call and response from the boards. She'd carry on for some time, with others joining in. Pretty soon, almost everyone in the church would be on their feet, shouting and praising the Lord. The pianist made the piano moan as he stomped his feet to the rhythm. The pulsating sound of coordinated clapping folded into what sounded like a practiced syncopation emanating from every corner.

Without warning, someone would belt out a loud scream and leap into the air or fall to the floor. Another would pass out and roll across the floor from side to side as the ushers covered her with white sheets to avoid indecent exposure. Some foamed at the mouth, while others spoke in tongues. It was an awesome sight, filled with an energy one had to experience to understand. But it was a normal occurrence for us. Tony and I tried to figure out how two eight-year-olds could participate without being accused of playing with the Holy Spirit.

One Sunday, we decided if MinyNar got happy, we would get happy, too, by imitating her. When Rev. Obadiah reached his high point in the sermon, the moans and groans began. Then a scream went out like a signal of preparation. Someone began shouting. Then someone else ran around the church, arms flailing. Then, at last, there she was. MinyNar hurled her enormous body from the pew, speaking in tongues and flailing her hands and arms. Tony and I, sitting on either side of MinyNar, leaned back and looked at each other with an all-knowing glance; it was our time to have some fun. We jumped up and down and began stomping, saying, "Thank you, Jesus! Thank you, Jesus!" We threw our hands in the air and over our heads, bowing our heads and shaking our bodies, pretending to be in the Spirit.

In the middle of one of MinyNar's hand-swinging motions, we quickly became acquainted with her devastating aim. She slapped us both across the mouth simultaneously with perfect precision. But as quickly as she'd swung both arms, catching us right where she'd intended, she slipped back into the Holy Ghost. We realized the Holy Ghost took short breaks. We never tried that again. And she never spoke of the incident. We assumed she didn't remember because the Holy Ghost had stepped in and disciplined us for her.

Another thing Tony and I enjoyed about church was the fact that everyone was expected to be a cheerful giver. As school-aged children, we had to rely on the adults to make sure we had our church money. So before we left home on Sunday mornings, we received some loose change, which never amounted to more than a dollar between the two of us. We always had a business meeting before leaving home, ensuring we were on one accord as to how much of our Sunday offering we'd leave in Rev. Obadiah's offering plate because we had plans to visit Mr. Sam Jones's candy store. Sunday was the only time we had money, and penny candy and cookies were far more important than giving our money to somebody neither of us thought needed it. We made sure we decided on the same amount, so if we got caught, the punishment would be the same. Our system worked well; we never got caught, although MinyNar often asked us where we got money for candy and cookies. Our response was that we'd found it or one of the adults had given it to us for going to the store for them or some other lame lie.

Being a child who was often hungry, living in MinyNar's house on Saturday nights and Sundays was a blessing. Sunday meals were a feast of delicious foods that we'd begun preparing on Saturday evenings. There was to be no cooking on the Sabbath. Sundays yielded some good eating. The meal was a family affair and usually enjoyed at supper, which was after the Sunday church dinner. Everyone took part in the preparation. On Saturday night, MinyNar divvyed up the responsibilities of cleaning vegetables, peeling potatoes, cutting pickles, and peeling boiled eggs. Mr. Eel would get a ham from the smoke shed, too. MinyNar did all the cooking, and Tony and I churned the old-fashioned homemade ice cream maker to make ice cream. We were proud of our contribution. We got to make two kinds of ice cream, either vanilla, chocolate, strawberry, banana, or peach. MinyNar made ham, fried chicken, biscuits, cornbread, collard greens, string beans or cabbage, corn on the cob, potato salad, macaroni and cheese, tomato pudding, chocolate cake, and some kind of pie. The flavor depended on the mood she was in that night. We drank iced tea or Kool-Aid and, of course, had our homemade ice cream. The meals varied from time to time but not that much. It didn't matter to me. I was being fed like I was royal blood.

Securing a chicken from the chicken coop was also one of Mr. Eel's jobs. Tony and I never missed this event. We watched as Mr. Eel prepared to ring the chicken's neck while it screamed in anticipation. When the head came off, we ran to stay clear of the jumping chicken, who would move through the air and over our heads, splattering blood everywhere until the final nerves in its body collapsed. Mr. Eel would immerse the chicken into a large pot of scalding water, where its feathers loosened. Then he plucked the chicken clean and prepared it for cooking. All parts were cooked, except the head, which went to the dogs. Even the feet were used to make delicious chicken feet stew or dumplings.

MinyNar's house, like many southern structures, stood high off the ground on bricks. It was high enough for Tony and me to bend just a bit and walk right under the house, where we went many times to play. There were lots of chickens in the backyard and one ornery red rooster who was meaner than Bad Leroy Brown. He constantly fought the other roosters. He'd take their food and bristle up at anyone who came near his domain. I was afraid of chickens because of that rooster.

One day, while we were playing under the house, he got out of the chicken coop and began chasing Tony and me as usual. Tony was able to get from under the house and make it to the front porch, but I froze, too afraid to move. That ornery son of a gun attacked me. He took long, graceful steps toward me, poking his head out first with his breast pushed proudly outward, preparing for attack. All I could do was defensively raise my hands and arms to my face to protect myself. His red feathered head bobbed back and forth as he pecked me incessantly. Then came his spurs. He was a bully! I tried to scoot backward on my butt, but the ground was too rough for my bottom. Girls didn't wear long pants too often. I had only my shorts on and a top. I was caught in his fury, and he loved every minute of it. Luckily, I had my defenses up, so I wasn't as badly scarred as I could have been. He drew blood but no deep wounds. He wore me out. I screamed, and my mom came running to see what happened. When she arrived, I was shaking and crying. She shooed the rooster away with a small tree branch and beckoned for me to come from under the house. Soon after, she made it all better.

I've been afraid of chickens ever since. The only solace I received was when it was time for that old, mean-ass rooster to meet his fate on the chopping block. Tony and I made it a special occasion. We had ice cream cones and stood around in the backyard waiting for it to happen. Mom grabbed that sucker by the neck, put his little red head down on the chopping block, and we listened as he lost his cussed disposition and begged for mercy. The sound he made before the axe met his neck was music to our ears. He yelped sorrowfully, but we felt no pity for him. Tony and I jumped up and down, imitating his jerking body as it bounced and flew around the yard until he dropped. I couldn't wait to get him on the dinner table so I could have the last laugh, but Mom said he wouldn't be good eating because roosters were often the toughest of the chickens, with a gamey flavor. However, to satisfy me, she served him up in a pot of stew. I never enjoyed sinking my teeth into something so much. It was the sweet taste of revenge.

CHAPTER 6

Saratoga—One Good Memory

Mini, one of MinyNar's daughters, had a dozen children. Seven of them were girls, and I slept in their bed on some weekends—four of us at the top and four at the bottom. It was fun for me because I was still an only child at the time, so being with other children was always fun since I was forced to move around a lot. And they were supposedly my cousins. We all piled up on the same bed, with no blankets, only coats, bedspreads, and sheets to shield us from the biting winter air that loomed into each of the heatless rooms during the night. Our bodies absorbed as much of the cold air as possible. The sleeping arrangement worked well to help generate warmth, unless it was one of those nights when I wet the bed. Steam would rise from the wet spot, and when I turned over, it caused the cold air to marry the pee, creating a wave of chilliness that everyone hated.

"Don't move!" they'd yell. "Stop fanning the covers!"

But it would be too late. I was a constant bedwetter, and it upset my cousins because the room was already cold, and the pee made it colder. No one wanted to use the outhouse late at night in the dead of winter, so there was a slop jar in the room for us to relieve ourselves. They became angry when I didn't get up during the night to make use of it. They thought I'd made a lazy decision to just lie there and pee in the bed. They, nor anyone else, understood that I had developed nocturnal enuresis, which I later learned was a direct result of the repeated childhood trauma in my life. Out of ignorance, I was referred to as "lazy bones," "pissy cat," "piss box," and "pissy ass."

The two oldest of Mini's girls were Corinne and Margaret. Despite my nighttime condition, they loved having me around. And when Tony and I went to school, Corinne and Margaret always accompanied us. Tony was in a different class, but Corinne, Margaret, and I were all in Miss Gray's class. On the first day I arrived at Ida Easter Elementary School, my cousins made it a point to dutifully inform Miss Gray that I was their responsibility, and I had to stay with them wherever they went. Margaret and Corinne were about one year apart in age, but they were two and three years older than me; yet all three of us were in second grade. I learned that Margaret and Corinne had been retained a few times. When I inquired why, the response was swift: "They dumb!"

In Miss Gray's classroom, we sat at desks constructed for two students, with chairs attached to each. The tops of the desks were smooth, with a long pencil groove. The rest of the room was decorated with the traditional large, gray, square-shaped alphabet wall charts, which hung over the chalkboard, with examples of cursive capital and lowercase letters. On another wall, a large calendar hung with colored oval-shaped pictures of presidents, ranging from George Washington to Dwight D. Eisenhower.

Corinne slid into one of the desks first and gestured for me to get in. I did, since the desks were designed for two people. I was small, so I fit in right next to her. Then, to my surprise, Margaret tried to squeeze in next to me, sandwiching me in. It was so tight that I was pushed against the back of the desk and their arms met, so I was barely visible. I squirmed, trying to free myself, but they were much too big for me to get any leverage or relief. Miss Gray promptly intervened, informing them that it was all right for me to sit in one of the vacant seats. But they didn't want to hear it. They promptly reminded her that they had been left in charge of me. So Margaret tried to move to the edge of the seat to give me a little more space, but she fell to the floor. When she got up, she moved to the vacant seat while rolling her eyes at Corrine. I realized they were fighting over who would get to sit next to me. I asked why, and they said because I was like a doll.

They argued over everything that had to do with me. When no consensus could be reached, they decided they'd both "keep" me. They fussed over me, rubbing my face and playing with my hair. They asked the other children, "Ain't our cousin cute?"

I later learned they fussed over me because they were unhappy with the way they looked. They wanted light skin and "good" hair. They thought I had what they wanted, only I didn't know I had anything but a hard life. I was poorer and needier than the two of them combined, so I wasn't aware of my skin color or the texture of my hair. I worried too much about the meals I'd miss if I wasn't in place at someone's home when suppertime came. They at least had a place they called home and daily meals.

Even though Corinne and Margaret had a place to live, none of us had indoor plumbing. I went to use the outhouse one day back at MinyNar's house, and I climbed onto it with my feet planted squarely on either side of the opening, squatting over the hole, careful not to sit or allow my bottom to touch the surface. I proceeded to do my business and cleaned myself with a brown paper bag. We'd been taught to rub the bag together to soften it before wiping. Upon releasing the piece of soiled paper bag into the opening, I noticed an area I had forgotten to clean. So, as I had been taught, I revisited the area and tried desperately to wipe away what appeared to be feces. But it was still there. I stretched to lean my head between my legs to see better. Closer examination revealed that what I thought was residue from improper cleaning was really a long, pink roundworm dangling from my rectum. Horrified, I jumped from the toilet top, somehow stepping out of my panties, and took off running from the worm. He kept up with me, though, moving as fast as I did. He wouldn't leave, and I couldn't shake him. The faster I ran, the tighter he held on. My mind was playing awful tricks on me; I was sure I could feel him whipping around like a jockey slapping his horse to make him giddy up. I couldn't stop. I had to outrun him to get rid of him. I didn't understand that I needed to stop and have the damn thing yanked from my butt.

I was moving so quickly that when my mom saw me running past the house, she thought something was chasing me. She leaped from the front porch and joined the race, trying to catch me to see what the haste was about. When she finally caught me, she tried holding me still by the shoulders, but I kept wiggling and twisting.

"I got to go! I got to go! It's gonna get me!" I yelled.

She forced me to stand still. "What's gonna get you?"

"The worm in my butt!"

She realized the problem and knew exactly what to do. She instructed me to bend over, and she gently removed the worm just by pulling on it.

Worms—just one more condition of being poor and impoverished.

Despite MinyNar's tough exterior and need to know everything that went on in her home, she wasn't as in the know as I needed her to be. Jack, Mom, and I shared a bedroom. On days when Mom had to work in the fields, it meant an early rise for her. She was usually up and ready to leave the house between four and five a.m. to catch an old ragged school bus that had been converted into a field hands' bus. She would stay away all day, not returning until around six p.m. Once her day got going, everyone else began stirring. And like clockwork, I was awakened by Jack when he moved his large body over to mine, wrapping his big hands around my tiny body to begin his daily routine of pleasuring himself by molesting me.

The image of Mr. Fetch sprang into my mind, and I felt the same way as back then, but, now, I was two years older, and it made me feel sick to my stomach. I thought he was my biological father, my protector. I thought he was my mother's husband. But my thoughts meant nothing to him. He gyrated his large frame against mine and forced his finger into my little opening while kissing me on the neck. This went on almost every morning, except on the nights I spent at his sister Mini's house with Corinne, Margaret, and the others.

I wasn't free of that predator until he was finally arrested and sent to prison, which made our stay in Saratoga with MinyNar short lived. According to Mom, she'd had words with MinyNar. She said MinyNar told Mom to "go shit and jump over it backwards," whatever that meant. But the directive backfired on MinyNar because Mom said, before she could reply, I retorted, "No, *you* go shit and jump over it backwards." It was an unexpected and unacceptable response, especially coming from a child.

MinyNar began to plan our exit strategy. She went into her secret closet, got down on her knees, and began chanting, "Lord, buke that devil outta my house." She continued until Mom finished gathering our little brown bag of nothings and moved on.

We left Saratoga.

My mom later told me the real reason MinyNar was angry was because Jack was arrested because Mom pressed charges against him after one of his brutal beatings. Mom was 5'5" and weighed about 125 pounds. Jack weighed about 250 pounds and was approximately 6'4" and built like a football player. He and Mom had been arguing over me. Mom wanted to leave the house, but Jack wanted me to remain there with his family. In hindsight, I realize he wanted to continue his sick morning ritual of molesting the child he thought to be his biological daughter. Our departure would change the course of his plan. My mom's resistance resulted in him punching her in her mouth so hard she began to gag. MinyNar ran in to see what happened. She saw Mom spitting out blood and a tooth. Jack had knocked her top front four teeth out, and three went down her throat. The other one lay on the floor covered in blood. She later reminisced about the incident, saying her teeth went down her throat like a pair of dice hitting the back surface of a wall during a crapshoot. MinyNar encouraged Mom to call the police, and when she did, she became enraged at the nerve of her own daughter-in-law pressing charges against her son. He was taken away in handcuffs. But no medical attention was ever provided for Mom. Instead, MinyNar began ranting and raving about it being my mom's fault.

We went back to Pond Town. Miss Sadie took us in temporarily because Mom was, again, between jobs. We had no money, so our stay was short because Mom couldn't contribute monetarily. She said I would need to move again. I was heartbroken; I had been looking forward to spending more time with Miss Gray in Ida Easter Elementary School. I was disappointed about leaving her because I had learned that teachers were the givers of knowledge, and new knowledge took me to my secret place. I hadn't been given an opportunity to spend enough time with Miss Gray and see how she could further nourish my intellect. She hadn't enough time to show me just how much she cared about teaching me what was inside those books I so loved. What kind of school would I now attend? I was sick to my stomach and felt like I would faint.

CHAPTER 7

New Parents

One Saturday, without warning, Mom introduced me to a childless couple, Miss Mable and Mr. Ray. They came into Miss Sadie's second big house, which was located in Pond Town on Hunter Street. I never knew their last name. When Mom told me about them, I thought I'd have more time to be with her before leaving with them. But no sooner than we were introduced, Mom said, "Phyllis, you gonna stay with Mable and Ray for a while, okay?" as if I had a say in the matter. "It won't be long, I promise. I just ain't got the money to keep you right now. Anyway, they some nice people."

"Ma, do I have to go? I don't want to leave you again. Please. I promise I won't be no trouble to you. I'll be real good. Please. Just don't make me go away again."

"I have to. I can't feed you, and I ain't got nowhere for us to stay right now," my mom said in a trembling, saddened tone. "And, Phyllis, you ain't been a bad girl. You didn't do nothing wrong, honey. I just don't have a job right now. That's why I'm trying my best to find somewhere for you to stay where you can be safe and eat and go to school. You don't want me to send you away to a home or nothing, do you? And don't worry none. I'mma come get you as soon as I can. Stop crying. Come here."

My mom squeezed me and held me for a long time, as if it would be the last time she'd ever see me. I was afraid it would be. The warmth of her embrace felt like heaven. She kneeled in front of me so she was at eye level and pulled my frail little body into her again. I wished we could stay right there, in that time and space, forever. I think she wished it, too. I knew she loved me, but taking care of me was too hard for her right then. She knew my pain. Oddly enough, I knew hers too, and I tried to be a big girl and not cry. I held on for as long as I could, but I eventually began whimpering and crying uncontrollably.

"Where you gonna stay? I can stay where you gonna stay," I reasoned.

"No, you need to be where you can eat and go to school every day. You know how you love school. Mable and Ray will see to it that you go every day, so you won't have to miss anything. Won't you like that? And it won't be long. I'll be back to get you before you know it. I promise. Now be a good girl for me, okay?"

I had no verbal response. Instead, I continued crying inside and out. I couldn't understand what I had done to deserve this. Many of the children in the neighborhood were poor, too, but none seemed to have to get up and leave their homes as often as we did.

Life with my new parents was already in motion. They were outside waiting to take me away in their car. Mom came outside with me, holding my hand as she walked me to the car with another brown paper bag of nothings I had acquired from different people. I struggled, pulling back and hoping my resistance would somehow change the situation. But to no avail. Once inside, I got on my knees in the backseat and looked back to see my mom in the distance. I watched, waved, and cried until I couldn't see her waving anymore. A mixture of salty tears and snot dripped onto my clothes, but I didn't care. I longed for my mom already. I wanted her badly. It seemed I never quite got enough of her. And now, she was only an imaginary figure in a wide space on the road where nothing else existed.

My head pounded like a jackhammer. I wanted it to stop. I was all too acquainted with the kind of hurt that penetrated the soul and took control of everything. It was one of the most painful ordeals I'd ever experienced. The separation left me numb. I yearned for my mom. I needed her love. I wanted to be with her, even if it meant being hungry and homeless. As the car moved on, I sat still, crying, moaning, and whimpering softly, wondering what this new experience would be like.

I had learned to deal with leaving as a part of life, but I didn't like it. It seemed it had to be that way for me to eventually return to my mother. The only solace I had were the kisses and hugs I'd receive upon her return that were like a sweet balm in Gilead. God, I loved her so much! She was so beautiful to me.

I hoped Mr. Ray wouldn't be like Mr. Fetch or Jack. I hoped he hated little girls and wouldn't do the things they had done to me. I hoped I could be invisible and he wouldn't notice that I was a cute little girl with big legs.

As it turned out, they were a nice couple. They had a nice apartment and offered security for an eight-year-old girl. My initial reaction to Miss Mabel was fear. She was nice enough, but there seemed to be something wrong with her mouth. Her top lip was turned up almost to the tip of her nose and her bottom lip was turned down almost to the middle of her chin. The outsides of her lips were dark brown and huge. The inside was bubblegum pink. Her teeth protruded, causing her mouth to have an apparent opening right in the center. Her lips looked as if she had been repeatedly beaten in the mouth. I think they looked that way, in part, because she smoked excessively and drank heavily. My mother said she had also been beaten a lot by her first husband. But those curled lips live vividly in my mind, even today. Yet, she was one of the nicest caretakers I ever had, especially for a non-blood relative.

Once I was enrolled in school, the other children in the neighborhood teased me about my "new mother," joking that her husband must've used her lips for a punching bag. She had what we called a coal-black complexion, with very smooth skin, and she was short, with a small build and muscular bowlegs. She had short, cropped hair and a cross between a bounce and a skip when she walked.

Mr. Ray was light skinned. In fact, I thought he was a white man when I first saw him. He may have been bi-racial. He had jet black, straight hair that was combed to the back of his head, with a part on the right side. He was a slender man and not much taller than Miss Mabel. But his face was pleasant, unlike Miss Mabel's. Despite her unsightly looks, they doted on each other and on me, too.

The entry to the house was around back and up one flight of creaky wooden stairs, situated over one other family that lived downstairs. There was a backyard, where I often played, either by myself or with a new friend named Ruby. She was a bit older than me and had lived in the neighborhood since birth. She was nice and was allowed to come over often to play with me. She had nice toys and my favorite, paper dolls. When Miss Mabel learned how much I liked those paper dolls, she made sure I had my own. Boy, was I happy! I had my own paper dolls.

Ruby had books, too. And occasionally, when I was given permission to play at her house, I would sit in her room on the floor in the lotus position and thumb through pages and pages of her beautiful books with all the lovely pictures and words. I used to copy some of those stories on pieces of paper and take them with me, so I could re-read them later to my paper dolls while they sat obediently as my new students. It helped me forget about Miss Gray for the time being.

Miss Mabel and Mr. Ray didn't live too far from Pond Town; however, they lived far enough away that I would have to change schools again. But changing schools was the least of my worries. Changing households made me wonder if my mother remembered to tell Miss Mabel about my problem. How would I tell her? Would they beat me? *What should I do?* Then it happened. I woke up after my first night in my new home. I sat up on the sofa bed and looked Miss Mabel straight in the eyes.

She asked, "What's wrong?"

"Nothing," I said, but she was smarter than that.

"Come over here," she urged. "Get out of the bed."

"I can't."

"Why?"

I was silent and hung my head in shame, afraid to tell her what I had done. I hoped she'd make some intelligent guesses or play a game of twenty questions, or something. But she didn't. Finally, she figured it out. "Oh, you peed in the bed?"

Mom used to promise a spanking if I wet the bed, although she never followed through. And I often heard friends talk about how they were spanked for wetting the bed. I expected the same. I began to cry loud and hard. I knew I would be beaten.

But Miss Mabel was the nice lady I perceived her to be. She said, "Oh, don't worry none about that. It could happen to anybody. And stop crying. I'm not gonna beat you."

That was good news. I had gotten through it that time, but I needed my mother because Miss Mabel had to know there would be a next time, and a next time, and a next. How would I pull it off? I couldn't worry about that because there was nothing I could do about it.

Mr. Ray tried to help me. He would promise me a quarter for every morning I woke up dry. It happened a couple of times, but mostly, I lost. They didn't understand the problem. I didn't either. But they never spanked me or scolded me about it. Their understanding was one of the reasons school was less stressful, and I slept comfortably every night. But I woke up each morning with my heart racing because I didn't know what would happen when they learned, again, that I had wet their sofa bed.

I got used to their place fast. The house was small, with only one bedroom, a kitchen, living room, and bathroom. I slept in the living room on the sofa. They had lots of food, so I was well fed and Miss Mabel would sit at the kitchen table and have discussions with me, asking how my day went, what I did in school, and what I wanted for dinner. We even talked about what I would wear to school and other girly things that other adults didn't often discuss with me. Miss Mabel was different. I enjoyed the large steel-legged chrome kitchen table with the pearl-gray shiny top. It was rectangular, with two matching red and pearl-gray chairs. The seats were thick and comfortable. There was a window near the table, with the customary stiffly starched clean curtains. A small gas stove was in the corner next to the sink. The second room was the living room, and it was incredibly small, with a TV, a coffee table, a tall gray wardrobe, and a sofa bed. The sofa was brown and plaid, with big buttons in different sections. Nightly, they removed the coffee table and put it in the kitchen so my bed could be opened. That was wonderful—my own sleeping quarters.

Mr. Ray and Miss Mabel's room was even smaller than the others. Their bed was huge. It was customary to stack mattresses on top of each other, and they did. There were at least three. I was little, so

I had to climb on from the foot by stepping on a black trunk that rested at the foot of the bed. Sometimes Mr. Ray would pick me up and put me on the bed. That was fun because he always handled me like I thought a father was supposed to handle his child. I trusted him, and he never gave me a reason not to. When I got the opportunity, I slept in their bed, usually on Saturday and Sunday nights, because if company came, they would need to sit on the sofa. In their room, other than the bed and a trunk, there was a dresser with a big mirror that hung on the wall and was held by a piece of wire. It was a comfortable place to raise a child. I was beginning to like it, and I liked Miss Mabel and Mr. Ray. They were good people, who deserved to have a child of their own. And I believe they are one of the reasons I have lived my adult life with a lack of bitterness and a spirit of caring for other people's children.

CHAPTER 8

Lessons Learned

When Monday morning came around, Miss Mabel enrolled me into Andrew J. Brown Elementary School on Smith Street. She had to take care of everything since I was being enrolled into a new school in the middle of the school year. She completed her business and I was led to my classroom. It was a colorful room facing Smith Street. I walked into the class and was greeted by Miss Cross, my new second grade teacher. She had a honey blonde skin tone, long hair, and she was pretty and pleasantly plump. She was also nice. She accepted me and made me feel welcome. She instructed the students to say hello to me, and I said hello, waving to everyone as I was led to my seat.

There was a boy named Earnest Boone in my class, and he was nuts. He always did daring, nutty things. Once, when Miss Cross left the classroom to go across the hall to talk to another teacher, Earnest asked us to dare him to jump out of the window. Well, that sounded exciting, so we dared him to jump. We stood on the desks and leaned out the window so we could watch crazy Earnest. He climbed up on the window ledge, perched himself like a leapfrog and said, "See y'all!"

We gasped. Luckily, our classroom was only on the second floor. We leaned out further to see if we could spot him. We yelled in sheer delight at the sight of Earnest struggling in the flowerbed near the side of the building, trying to pick himself up. He looked up at us and started waving and laughing.

Somehow, Miss Cross heard all the commotion, and she frantically bolted into the room. "What's going on in here? Where's Earnest?"

Somebody yelled, "Earnest out there!" pointing toward the window.

But I don't think it registered because she continued inquiring. In a frightened voice, she asked again, "Where is Earnest? What happened?"

Everybody began telling her at the same time.

"Take your time. Slow down. Now, what happened? Where is Earnest?"

Everyone couldn't talk at the same time, so most of us pointed at the window. Miss Cross's mouth fell open. She rushed over to the window and looked outside. By then, Earnest was just standing there.

"Earnest Boone, what are you doing out there?" she yelled.

"Hi, Miss Cross," said Earnest. "I ain't doing nothing."

"You get in here right now before I skin you alive."

"Yes, ma'am."

We all waited to see what kind of justice he would get. I learned early that Earnest was always in some kind of trouble, so it was nothing new for any of us to witness. He sauntered into the room as if nothing happened, whistling with his hands in his pockets. He had dirt all over his clothes, and a purple tulip from the flowerbed was stuck in the side of his shoe. Miss Cross met him in the hallway then followed him into the room. She shook him and scolded him all the way to the cloakroom. Once they made it to the cloakroom, we all knew what would happen next. Miss Cross whipped him good with a paddle. He never cried. We could hear her say, "You're never going to forget this day, Earnest Boone." He probably never did. I didn't either, but it wasn't because she hadn't made him cry. It was because I was all too familiar with what punishment looked like and never wanted to cross Miss Cross.

The punishment didn't appear to move Earnest one bit. He left the cloakroom, walking in front of Miss Cross, smiling at some of us and making faces at those of us who laughed at him. He was a real character. But he sure knew how to infuriate Miss Cross. I never knew anyone in my short time there as a student who could anger her the way he did. Her face would turn red like the white ladies who lived on Day Street, on the other side of the tracks, when they saw us coming down "their" street, using it as a shortcut to get uptown. Their faces turned red that same way, and they'd scream at us, "Niggers! Get off this street!" We would immediately start running because we knew if someone was outside and spotted us, the dogs would follow. I think those dogs were trained to chase black folks only, and the attack word was probably "nigger." That word always seemed to send the dogs into a frenzy. Earnest Boone made Miss Cross angry enough to sic something on him, but she never called him a name.

I had my first art lesson in Miss Cross's class. She would have us take a piece of string and drop it on the surface of a sheet of unruled paper and trace over the string wherever it fell. We repeated the process until the page was covered with what we called a string design. She instructed us to color our designs with crayons. I made a beautiful design that I gave to Miss Mabel. She hung it up and reminded me often how lovely it was. Miss Mabel was building my self-esteem one day at a time.

That art lesson was my initial experience of matching colors and making designs. I was interested and wanted more. It gave me a feeling of belonging. But Miss Cross taught me something else, too. I learned to play my first real game: pick up sticks. Those two activities won me friends while living with Miss Mabel and Mr. Ray. But Ruby and I were already friends, and she walked me home until I learned my way on my own. One day, Ruby stopped by to pick me up for school. I was excited because no one had ever cared enough about me to pick me up for school. I was also excited because Miss Mabel had given me my first pocketbook. It was an old pocketbook that she no longer used, but it was mine now and new to me. I was eager to show it to Ruby. I even opened it to show her all the goodies I had inside. The pocketbook was a black miniature patent leather version of a 50s oval-shaped overnight bag, the ones that flipped open, with a mirror in the top inside flap. And it had double carrying handles. Ruby complimented me on my "new" bag. She said it was the nicest pocketbook she'd ever seen, and she wished she had one. I told her she could borrow it sometime if she really liked it that much. We decided she should only borrow it when we didn't have school, though, because the kids at school would see her with it and know it was mine.

I left home that morning excited about my school day and as proud as a peacock. I owned something. On the way home that afternoon, Ruby and I encountered some kids on the other side of the street who decided it was a good day to be cruel to me. "Hey, yellow girl! Where'd you get that ugly grandmamma pocketbook from?" they yelled and erupted into laughter.

I didn't say anything, not because I was ignoring them, but I was afraid of them. They were much bigger than we were. Ruby knew them and said they were in a higher grade.

They continued. "I know that's your mama's grandmama's pocketbook."

Ruby said, "Don't pay them any mind. My mama told me I couldn't play with them, anyhow. They ain't nothing but troublemakers."

I tried to forget what they were saying. I started telling Ruby about all the nice things I had included in my pocketbook. She already knew what was in there because I had told her before, but she was patient. Before I could finish telling her, a boy ran across the street and snatched it from me. He threw it on the ground, and all my things fell out. I kneeled and began picking them up and started crying.

The boy began stomping my things and laughing. "Look, y'all. Watch this," he said to the kids across the street.

Ruby bent down to help me pick up the contents of my pocketbook. All the other children continued laughing at me. They enjoyed every minute of my pain and humiliation. It all happened right downstairs from where I lived. I grabbed my stuff, thanked Ruby, and ran upstairs, crying. I told Miss Mabel what happened, and she hugged me hard and told me to stop crying. To make me feel better, she vowed to meet me from then on when it was time for school to be out. I agreed. I loved that pocketbook, but it couldn't belong to me anymore. It had caused too much pain. I neatly opened my heart and placed the injured memories somewhere in the back with all the other pain stored there. I never took that pocketbook out of the house again.

CHAPTER 9

Balancing Good, Bad, and the Church

Miss Mabel allowed Ruby and me to visit Morgan Memorial Library at 443 W. Washington Street, which was close by, and we were both old enough to go by ourselves, so we walked there after school one day. I had seen the large structure many times during my short stay with Miss Mabel. She took that route when we went shopping at the local market. I'd look out the window at the big brick building and dream about all the books inside. It was constructed of red bricks, and it had huge white Doric columns in front and two large white doors with gold handles. I longed for the day I could visit there because I loved books, even though I didn't own one, nor did I have access to any books, except school books and the Bible wherever my mother set up house. I had seen many beautiful children's books in my classroom, and I wanted to go to a place where there was nothing but books. It would be great to just go inside and see all the wonderful books, with their words and pictures. Finally, I was going to do just that.

Ruby and I approached the great steps of the awesome building. My heart began to pound. What an experience it would be. When we reached the large doors and pulled them open to go inside, we looked to our left and saw little white children and their mothers standing patiently, waiting for the woman behind a circular desk to check out books for them. The place was quiet, and our presence made it even quieter. Immediately, everything came to an abrupt halt, and the talking voices were suddenly mute. The lady behind the desk stopped what she was doing and hastily moved from her place and walked right over to where Ruby and I stood. She wore cat-eye glasses that curled at the ends, and she had on a starched pale green dress with a large white bow at the neck and a big patent leather belt.

She stood in front of us with her hands on her hips. "And just what do y'all want?" Her words were deliberate and toxic.

"We came to look at some books and maybe take some home to read," I said.

"Oh no, you're not getting any books from here. So just turn around and get your little black selves out of here right now."

We turned around sadly with a feeling of defeat and walked to the door as the woman held it open for us, pointing outside. She couldn't wait to close the door behind us. If we hadn't moved so quickly, the door may have hit us on the heels. I didn't visit another public library until many years later.

My fondest memory at Andrew J. Brown School was when I was given a part in a play called *A Frog Went a Courtin',* and I was the little yellow chick. I had to wear a yellow dress. Miss Mabel discussed it with my mother, and either my mother found the money from somewhere and purchased that yellow dress for me or someone gave it to her; I didn't care because on the night of the play, my dreams came true. I was a yellow chick standing on the stage in front of a crowd. But the only one in that crowd that made a difference to me was my mom. She'd promised me she would be there, and she was. I didn't acknowledge my part until my mom acknowledged her baby. I waved at her until she waved back at me, then I carried on with my performance, and I remembered all my lines.

Miss Mabel and Mr. Ray, like many people during that time, worked for the weekends. They worked hard and played even harder. When Friday night came, they were ready to P-A-R-T-Y. They partied from Friday night until Sunday. We frequently visited friends who lived in the large white house at the top of a dead-end street on a steep hill. I loved going to that house with Mr. Ray and Miss Mabel because I could listen to the music on the piccolo and dance until it was time to go home. The latest dance was the peppermint twist, and I could out twist everybody. The grown folks would sit around and clap, chant, and cheer me on. They kept putting dimes and quarters in the piccolo, playing tunes just to watch me dance with the other children. If the adults wanted to see me dance, they'd pay me for my talents. I was used to that. I used to get paid to dance when I lived in the Big House with Miss Sadie, too. If it were a really good night, there would be a competitor for me, and that meant double money because the winner took all. More times than not, I took all. My partner was usually some young whippersnapper who could dance just as well as I could, but our reasons for dancing were different. I danced harder and with more experience because I wanted the money. They were probably just dancing because they were told to be my partner. Not many of the children who knew my dancing skills wanted to compete against me. Those who had never danced with me before took the risk. When they did, they often quickly realized it was a losing battle and gave up right in the middle of a dance, walking away embarrassed. I was no joke. I took dancing seriously. I didn't have a lot of other things that many of the children my age had, so I overcompensated with what I did have. Dancing was one of those things.

Sometimes we stayed until late into the night, till one a.m. or three a.m., depending on how the party was going. If there was some gambling going on and Mr. Ray was winning, we'd stay even later. The owner of the house never minded because as long as someone was in the house, he'd make money from the songs playing on the piccolo, the gambling, and illegal alcohol sales. They bought brown liquor from the ABC store as well as corn liquor, beer, and cheap wine. The party was on every weekend, with dancing and chicken and pig feet dinners. I can still remember the crispy fried chicken sandwiches, too. The chicken lay between two pieces of Sunbeam white bread, soaked in chicken grease. We enjoyed that greasy chicken and bread. Weekends were social gatherings to which we all looked forward. And it helped me not think so hard about my mom.

Church wasn't a part of my life anymore. Mr. Ray and Miss Mabel didn't go to church, and they certainly didn't make me go. Other than weekend excursions at one of the big houses, the only other socializing we did was visiting friends of theirs, and the visits were reciprocated. Sometimes we'd all eat together during the visit and sometimes not. These were good times for me, with plenty of food, a social life, security, school, and two people who adored me.

Eventually, my mother got a job that brought her closer to me. Miss Mabel and Mr. Ray's house was right behind and diagonally from Mom's new place of employment, less than fifty feet away from its back door. She worked at The Pastry Shop. What a blessing! On weekends, my mother would sneak out of the shop every so often to see me, and every week day at four o'clock, when she got off work, she stopped upstairs at Miss Mabel and Mr. Ray's house and brought me day-old glazed donuts and cinnamon buns with white icing and raisins. When she could, she brought two of my favorites, French apple and blueberry pies. Having my mother that close to me made life with Miss Mabel and Mr. Ray even easier.

But I didn't remain with them much longer. My mom's job as a dishwasher and pastry maker earned her enough money to take me back to Pond Town with her. I continued attending Andrew J. Brown School in second grade for a while longer. I got up early every morning and walked to the bus stop, where I got on the city bus alone and rode to the other side of town to go to school. Mom wanted to remove me from Andrew J. Brown School and re-enroll me into Mary Estes Elementary School in Pond Town, where I had been a student in first grade, but I wouldn't hear of it. I was enjoying my education at Andrew J. Brown, and I loved Miss Cross, and she loved me. I didn't want to give up string art, pick up sticks, or reading the children's books in our classroom library. I just couldn't, so I pleaded with Mom and assured her if she showed me how to take the city bus, I would be fine. I would be a big girl and go straight to school by myself. I had to.

Miss Cross waited for me every day because she knew I was taking public transportation to school alone, and I was only eight years old, going on nine. I begged my mom to let me stay until the school year ended. She agreed as long as she still had a job, since she had to provide bus fare for me every day, which was around twenty cents round trip.

The white bus driver became friendly with me because I was his youngest passenger, and he began looking out for me. One day, there was only the two of us on the bus, and he slowed the bus down as we approached Planters Peanut Factory on Culloden Street. This wasn't unusual because there was a bus stop there and people either got on or off to go to work or head home. But this time, there seemed to be a great ruckus. Policemen and police dogs were everywhere. Dogs attacked the black people coming out of Planters Peanut Factory. Some of the men and women had handcuffs on, and the police were siccing dogs on them. Those who weren't handcuffed or attacked by the dogs began rocking the bus back and forth, but they weren't successful at overturning it.

The bus driver yelled to me, "Get down between the seats, and don't move until I say so."

I quickly obeyed and got as far down as I could. In an instant, there was a crash and glass spewed everywhere. Someone from outside had thrown a bottle at the bus and broke one of the windows. We were caught in the crossfire. The bus wasn't allowed to move because the street was blocked off by policemen, police cars, people who were being arrested, dogs, and others who stood on the sidelines yelling obscenities at the officers. It was a scary scene.

After what seemed like a long time, the bus driver finally came to the back of the bus to check on me. When he learned that I was okay, he instructed me to get up and return to my seat, and we drove off. I climbed onto my seat and got on my knees so I could watch the melee for as long as possible. I couldn't wait to get home to tell my mother about the experience. She listened and told me to slow down as I told the story with excitement. But Mom seemed to have something else more pressing on her mind.

When I finally shut up, I noticed her countenance. I held her face in my hands. "Mom, what's wrong?"

"The Pastry Shop no longer needs me. So when the funds dry up, you'll have to change schools and move again."

CHAPTER 10

A New Beginning and Ending

Next stop—Windsor, my mother's hometown, where I had several relatives. I moved in with Uncle Lescell and Aunt Clementine (pronounced Clem-in-teen). Windsor was a small, rural incorporated town in Isle of Wight County. At night, it got really dark, with no streetlights. Most roads were dirt roads, and the nearest store was miles away. We lived in our family's old homestead that once belonged to my great-grandmother, Julia Butler Eley. The old house was worn out, but because it was family property and had been in the family for many years, it was kept up for as long as possible.

The first room we entered in the house was significant to me because it became my bedroom. It was previously a den. The room was fine during the day, but scary for an eight-year-old at night. I slept on a backless sofa bed that faced a cuckoo clock positioned high on the wall directly in front of my bed. At night, it would frighten me. At precise intervals, the pendulum swung, making a tick-tock sound and causing the owl's white eyes to roll from side to side and pop its tongue out. "Cuckoo, cuckoo!" it screamed.

I hated when daylight slipped away. I was afraid of the dark and slept every night in that unlit room in fear of that damn clock. Over the front door rested a shotgun and on the left wall was a golf-ball-sized hole. One day, while sitting on the sofa bed, a long black snake slithered through that hole in the wall. I screamed bloody Mary, summoning Uncle Lescell. He bolted into the room and immediately snatched the shotgun, shooting the snake right there in that room. Then he hoisted it over the barrel of the gun and flung it out the door onto the ground.

Killing the snake was a good thing, but it didn't allay my fear much. So sleep never came easy, with the thought of more intrusions from critters, especially snakes. I always slept with my entire body tucked tightly under the covers, for fear of the clock chiming and a snake sliding into bed with me. Country living was new to me. There were all sorts of nocturnal sounds, like crickets, frogs, cicadas, and other undistinguishable creature noises that would frighten any eight-year-old. There was even talk of bears, although I never saw one while living with my uncle and aunt. My sleeping space gave me nightmares. For years, falling asleep meant dreaming about an uncontrolled fall into a snake pit or somehow being entangled in a bed of snakes. Aunt Clementine would explain it away by saying it was just the devil messing with me. I accepted that because I knew no better.

My aunt and uncle had no children together. Aunt Clementine had one adult son who lived with his maternal grandmother. But they loved me dearly. They were very nice to me, and I was their little girl.

Aunt Clementine knew of my condition, so she was prepared to deal with it right away. She thought the solution was to ration out the amount of water I drank during the day and gave me none at night. And when it was time for me to enroll in school, she reminded me of my water intake during school hours as part of her pep talk. I heard her, but I was more interested in the fact that I would be going off to school the very next day. I couldn't wait. I was even willing to go to sleep early and risk having my usual nightmare, just because I knew what the morning would bring.

Aunt Clementine drove the school bus, so I had the pleasure of riding with her every morning to everybody's house for pick up. My first morning was fun but seemed to take forever because I was anxious to start Georgia Tyler Elementary School and meet my new teacher.

At home, Aunt Clementine often held conversations with me, much like Miss Mabel. So it wasn't unusual for her to strike up a new one that morning. "You know your brother is coming down here this summer," she said nonchalantly.

"My brother? I don't have a brother," I said, astonished. Mom hadn't told me anything about a brother. "Where is he? Who does he live with? How old is he? Is he older than me? What does he look like? How is he my brother?"

I sent a barrage of questions across the aisle, each landing right in front of Aunt Clementine. She attempted to answer some of them. I wondered why no one had ever mentioned him to me; then Aunt Clementine tried to explain. "Your mother had a little boy, and his name is Michael. He lives in New Jersey with his mother."

I was confused and asked how we could have different mothers. She explained that Michael had been given to one of my great-aunts, Aunt Lois, who lived in Orange, New Jersey. She had no children and adopted Michael as an infant. I no longer cared for the details; I was excited to know I had a brother and he was older than me. It must have been Aunt Clementine's plan to tell me about him all along because when I expressed an interest in seeing him, she told me to look inside her purse and take out a picture of him. More confusion set in because I immediately recognized him, only I had been told he was my cousin. But it was okay. I'd learned the truth. I had a big brother!

Later that summer, I met Mike and we got to know each other. We played miniature golf with a toy set Aunt Clementine bought for me, and he taught me how to tie my shoelaces in a double bow. Mom later explained the true story of my brother. She was sixteen when she gave birth to him and couldn't take care of him—a fact confirmed by other family members. Through further family conversations, it was revealed that Aunt Lois had given Mom clear instructions: She was to give my brother to her, walk out of his life, and never come back. To ensure a future for him, Mom complied. But my brother later shared his understanding of the story. Aunt Lois told him Mom said she was going to the corner store to purchase a pack of cigarettes but never returned, leaving him there for her to care for him. So Mike grew up hating Mom and believing she walked out on him. It put a tremendous strain on their future relationship, which became the source of much pain for my mom.

As we approached the school, I heard children's laughter and saw lots of kids my age, younger, and older, running around and talking. I became giddy. Once we arrived and Aunt Clementine got me situated, I met Miss Gladys Chapman, and I loved her immediately. She was an old friend of the family and now my teacher. I kept her close to my heart because she was nice, and she spent quality time with me. She made sure I was caught up with the other students in class so my grades wouldn't fall behind. Sometimes, during our 10:30 recess, she helped me with work other students had already done. She let me read to her, too. I loved the attention and was excited about all the books she let me take home and the writing workbook pages to practice my penmanship.

She seemed to know that Georgia Tyler Elementary School was just another stopover for me. Although I was unaware at the time, I was part of a group of children in the school's mobility rate, which meant I was a transient student. She knew by training or intuition that she had limited time to integrate me into the life, culture, and curriculum of Georgia Tyler Elementary School. She had learned some things about me as a student and tried to prepare me for grade three by telling me I was a "smart little girl." I hung onto those words because they didn't come often enough. I worked hard for Miss Chapman. Her words remained with me and eventually found their way into my practice as a teacher many years later. Those words were magical, and I intended to use that magic with future children who also hadn't heard them often enough. Miss Chapman had unwittingly helped to plant the seed for my future and career. She was special to me, and I didn't want to let her down, so I never missed an assignment. But I, too, knew from experience that our relationship would be short lived, so I took in everything Miss Chapman had to offer.

Before I left Georgia Tyler, Miss Chapman taught me my right hand from my left. She said to always remember I held my pencil in my right hand. Miss Chapman made sure I went on my first field trip. It was to Williamsburg, Virginia. And she introduced me to May Day, an annual traditional spring holiday of dancing, singing, and sharing food around the May Pole. Miss Chapman also taught me how to do a curtsy. For the May Day program, I needed a white chiffon dress with a crinoline slip underneath, and Aunt Clementine saw to it that I had just what I needed. She told me I looked gorgeous—a compliment I had never heard before. I felt pretty, and I even smelled good because she made sure I had regular hot baths before bed each night. Aunt Clementine came to the May Day program to support me, and she was proud of my performance. Miss Chapman spent extra time helping me learn the song, "Georgie

Porgie Pudding Pie." The other children had been practicing it for some time. And on that day, I knew every word to the song.

As I unknowingly prepared to leave Georgia Tyler, I felt special and smart because Miss Gladys Chapman said so. I was ready academically for third grade but not emotionally. Forging another relationship with another teacher seemed emotionally draining, and I didn't know whether I would be up for the transition. I had no idea if my new environment would be supportive or how long we would be there.

I completed second grade after attending three schools and being successful at each. I didn't know if or when I would leave Aunt Clementine and Uncle Lescell. School was out; it was summertime, and I was still with them.

CHAPTER 11

The Thought of Death Cuts Deeply

My aunt and uncle were farmers, so at the onset of summer, I gained new experiences. Every morning during the summer months, we'd get up early and go to the fields; one of them drove the tractor and the other, the truck. It was fun interchanging who I rode with. Once the day reached eleven a.m. or noon, it was usually stifling, and I became thirsty. Sitting in the truck waiting for them every day taught me to create games to occupy myself while they worked. But the large gallon-sized pickle jar used for ice water from our well was also in the truck with me. I was warned not to have any of it because of my condition. However, I realized if I unscrewed the lid and drank some of the water, it wouldn't be missed because the ice melted and replenished it. When they came for water, Aunt Clementine would ask me if I had some. I'd say no, and she wouldn't know the difference. Then I'd ask if I could have a little bit. Aunt Clementine would say, "Well, you can have just a little bit because you know you'll pee in the bed tonight if you drink too much water." I accepted what she gave. Then when I wet the bed that night despite the rationing, Aunt Clementine would fuss a bit then ask me if I'd had more water than she'd given me, and I'd say no. No matter how little water she gave me, I'd still wet the bed.

Aunt Clementine clothed me well, too. I had cute, girly dresses, lace socks, shoes that fit, panties, and ribbons for my hair. We also ate great Sunday breakfasts. She made fried chicken legs, thighs, and wings, scrambled eggs, slices of homemade cheese, and hot homemade buttered biscuits with homemade jam and iced tea. Aunt Clementine put church back into my life. I became a Baptist by default. It was a family practice. And church was important because we didn't really see or talk to people too much during the week, since everyone lived so far from each other. In vacation bible school, I learned how to make pastel colored flowers. I also learned my first speech, which I had to recite in front of the entire church body at the end of vacation bible school in the gymnasium of Georgia Tyler Elementary School.

> *I stepped up on the stage one day, my heart went pita-pat.*
> *I heard someone say, "What little girl is that?"*
> *Phyllis Bivins is my name. Windsor is my station, heaven is my resting place, and God is my salvation.*

Aunt Clementine explained what the lines meant, and as young as I was, I somehow felt it gave me a sense of belonging.

Our only real way of communicating when not in church or school was via telephone, and Aunt Clementine warned me to be careful with the telephone because everyone had a party line, which was common for many years in rural areas. It could be dangerous because having a party line meant the local telephone circuit was shared by more than one subscriber, providing no privacy in communication. Anyone on the party line could pick up the phone and listen in on a conversation. The party line was an important source of entertainment as well as gossip. It also acquainted us all with what was going on in the surrounding area. And because people were not always discrete, trusting that no one was listening in on their conversation, unintended ears were often privy to information that was meant to be private.

After second grade had ended and before summer was over, Mom returned because she had found another place for us to live and wanted to take me back. But Uncle Lescell protested, and in an attempt to keep me with them, he imposed a caretaker fee on my mom. He knew she couldn't meet the demand but hoped it would deter her from moving me again because they were trying to give me some stability. He said before she would be allowed to remove me from the premises, she had to pay him for every day I'd spent there and for all the clothing they purchased for me. Mom said she didn't have the money, and if she gave him what she did have, there would be none left for our new place. But he insisted. I listened in silent contempt at the thought of not being able to reunite with my dear mother. However scant life was, I was indebted to her for always trying to secure our family unit and, more specifically, my survival. Uncle Lescell's browbeating sent Mom into a crazed frenzy. She was panic stricken and didn't know what to do. Of all the times she had left me in someone else's care, no one had ever protested when she came for me. But Aunt Clementine and Uncle Lescell had no children of their own, so my absence would represent a void in their lives.

I listened to every word of the conversation between Mom, Uncle Lescell, Aunt Clementine, and another great-aunt and uncle,

Savilla and Terry, who happened to be visiting that day. Mom led me by the hand and away from Aunt Clementine and the others to the back of the old homestead, where we sat on the steps together. She pulled me over to her and hugged me tight. It felt good but different.

"Phyllis, do you know what it means to die?" she asked.

"Yes," I responded.

"Well, I'm going to die. I'm going to kill myself if they don't let me have you back."

Tears rushed forward, washing my face in sadness. I cried hard, shaking my head and grabbing my mom, holding her in desperation, mulling over her words and contemplating what I'd do without her. The thought of her death cut deeply through my soul. My heart ached so much that I wanted to yank it from my chest. I was soaked in pain and anguish and didn't know what to do.

Finally, I said, "No, Ma. No! Please don't die. Please don't leave me. Please, Ma. I'll be good. Don't you love me, Ma? Please don't go away from me. I'll be scared, and I don't want you to leave me."

I tried desperately to hold her in place on those back steps. I kept pushing her down, but I was only a child. I couldn't contain her. The crisis of my mother's fate came so close that I felt the hand of death touching her. She got up and began walking back toward the front of the house. I ran to keep up with her and screamed at the top of my lungs as fear consumed me. "Uncle Lescell, help me! My mama trying to kill herself. She trying to jump down the well!"

She moved in and began climbing over the wall of the brick cylinder. The well, which had been the giver and sustainer of life, now stood as an open grave. My mother put both feet inside, her hands bracing the side of the round brown structure, and she began to remove one hand. My uncle ran from inside the house after hearing my screams and grabbed her under her arms, pulling her back. He went backward, and they both fell to the ground, she on top of him.

I was so grateful that I screamed, grateful that he'd heard and acted so quickly. Grateful that God had heard, too.

Aunt Clementine said, "Lescell, let her go. Forget the money. Give her the clothes we bought her, and let her take her child."

Aunt Savilla and Uncle Terry agreed with Aunt Clementine. That settled the matter. And I left that day, leaving behind the security of a home, a bed, three promised meals a day, a good school, church, family, new friends, and Miss Gladys Chapman's gentle way of teaching and loving.

I was filled with questions. Would my next home be comforting? Would my new teacher be like Miss Chapman? Would she understand me and love me the way she had? Mom knew how important school was to me. So no matter where we ended up, she'd secure a spot for me in a school somewhere. I learned that no matter what happened or where I went, there was always a school, and that gave me comfort.

CHAPTER 12

New Home, New Hope, New Hunger

This time, when we returned to Pond Town, we had a place to call our own, even though we were still struggling to escape the powerful grip of poverty. But I had secret hopes. We rented a house at 706 Orange Street. The houses weren't row houses, but they were close together. Each was a small three, four, or five-room house made of wood and cinderblock, with a wide gray cement porch with no steps. The houses were a move away from the typical house that often stood about two feet from the ground. These were flat to the ground, with small front yards and backyards large enough to plant gardens. We had a three-room apartment, with a living room, kitchen, bedroom, and an outhouse. There was little furniture, including a plastic sofa someone had discarded, which used to be white and now had long, open cracks and cuts, exposing dirty stuffed cotton with a variety of stains from being on the trash pile where we'd found it. It stood on three legs, propped against the wall as a substitute for a fourth leg. We had an old, worn sheet as a curtain in the front window and a ten-penny nail on either end of the wall substituting for a curtain rod to support the makeshift curtain and discourage passersby from peeking in. The kitchen had a sink but no running water and a four-eyed black and white old wood stove with duct tape along the feet of the stove to help extend its life. We had a small green table absent of most of its paint, with visible splinters and half of one of the boards missing, leaving a hole on one end. A single wooden kitchen chair with a missing spindle rested against the wall because it was too feeble to stand on its own. In our bedroom was a pretty pair of plastic curtains with reddish-pink roses on a white background that was shared by two windows. Mom stretched the pair to capacity, even though the sunlight and the evening streetlights always crept around the openings of those curtains. It was so cold during winter that the curtains would get hard and crack in places because the plastic was thin and cheap. There was a bed with a rusted frame and the lumpiest mattress imaginable. Sleeping on it was a methodical experience. Half-coiled wire stuck through the mattress from wear and tear and would stick, stab, and scratch at night if we didn't know our place. An old piece of cloth stood in as a bedspread. Both Mom and I slept on that bed. But that would soon change. Mom was pregnant.

Although we had nothing to start a garden, we sometimes depended on the neighbors' gardens, relieving them of some of their vegetables at night but only when we had nothing to eat. I often worried about food because there just never seemed to be enough. With no electricity or food, we could only keep food for a day or two before it spoiled. I was taught to check the bread before eating, and if we found mold, we tore away the molded part and ate the rest.

I later learned as an adult that my weight problem probably had a great deal to do with the way we ate when I was a kid. Mom would say, "You better eat everything on your plate and seconds if your belly will hold it because we don't know when our next meal is gonna be."

One hot summer day illustrated that point. I walked into the house after playing outside with the neighborhood kids and dutifully announced, "Ma, I'm hungry." I soon learned that we were at the onset of one of our dry spells for food.

"Baby, I ain't got nothing to eat right now. I'll get you something later," Mom said. When some time passed, I asked again, and she said, "Go down to Shirley's house; it's about time for dinner. She'll feed you."

So off I went to our neighbor's house. When Shirley fed her children, she fed me, too. I often made sure I was at Shirley and Burt's house to eat with their three children, Bessie, Tank, and Ronnie. When she called them in to eat, she would say, "Phyllis, you wanna come in and eat?" My answer was like a rehearsed line in an upcoming play: "Yes, ma'am."

Shirley and Burt were the ideal family. There was a mother, a father, and three children. They had adequate furniture in every room, and the children were always clean and well fed. They were also my friends and playmates.

Ronnie was short, resembling a cross between a little runt and Mr. Spock. His head was cigar shaped and his lips were in a permanent pucker, with an exaggerated philtrum. He always had a snotty nose and never wore shoes unless necessary, and his ears were pointy. When Ronnie ate, we always laughed at how much he enjoyed his food. He never waited for it to cool off. The food was so hot that when he ate, he would emit sounds that were a combination of crying, with tears streaming down his face, and humming, attesting to how good the food was. Although his parents hid their laughter, we often got in trouble for laughing at him.

Tank was the older brother. He had an unusual condition, too; however, we found no humor in it. His lips were practically fused together as a result of a childhood accident. When he was still a baby, not yet walking, his mother had left her mop water to answer the phone in another room. She heard a loud scream and rushed back to learn that he had drunk some of the water, which contained lye. The box of lye had the skull and crossbones label, which we were told to avoid because it meant poison or death. He was rushed to Obici Memorial Hospital, where doctors worked frantically to fix him. While he was fine internally, he was physically scarred forever. The solution of potassium hydroxide in the water had severely damaged his mouth, tongue, and gums, practically sealing his mouth shut. His tongue had become little more than a ball of pink flesh, and when his teeth finally grew in, they were shifted far back in his mouth where the front of his tongue would've been, causing his speech to be impaired. His lips were soldered from one side to the other, with only a surgically made opening large enough to fit two straws. As the years passed, he made repeated visits to specialists who were successful at opening his mouth more a little at a time. We never laughed at him because we didn't find his predicament funny. But an unanswered question loomed in our heads—Why didn't the doctors just cut his mouth completely open during one of those visits? No one ever answered our question.

Bessie was a chunky girl with very short hair, and the neighborhood kids used to tease her about it. She was special to me, so I never found anything funny about her size or her hair. She was my friend. But girls in the neighborhood who had longer hair sang a line from the song "Nearer to Thee" by Sam Cooke to taunt her as they pretended to comb through their hair. The objective was to try to get through the first line of the song's chorus before combing through someone's hair. The song had a moderate tempo, so it didn't take long to get through it; however, if the girl's hair was as short as Bessie's, they only got through the first two syllables. Some of the girls would run up behind her and quickly pull a comb through her hair two or three times. Each time, they would recite, "N-e, N-e, N-e" then laugh. Bessie would cry, and I would console her as best I could because I knew all too well what it felt like to be ridiculed. After all, she had consoled me on more than one occasion.

I was grateful to have Shirley and Burt and their kids in my life. I had three friends who accepted me for who I was and their parents, who made sure I ate when their children ate if I was present when supper was ready.

Other times when food was an urgent matter, I was sent door to door, shopping for meals at our neighbors' houses. I hated those moments, but they were necessary if we were going to eat. Sometimes Mom would send me with a note to avoid the embarrassment of having to ask for food. I'd go to Miss Sadie's Halladay Street house, where she lived when she wasn't running the Big House. I'd arrive with a note asking to borrow a few white potatoes. Then I'd stop at Miss Novella's house for a piece of streak-of-lean and streak-of-fat meat. She would often need an errand run, and I'd do it, which was her way of getting something for her generosity. But sometimes she would send me to the store and tell me to keep the change, which could be fifteen cents or so. Mom and I used the money to help buy dinner that day or the next. A loaf of bread was about seventeen cents, so that kind of loose change was significant. I stopped by Shirley's house for a cup of flour, and our next-door neighbor, Stella, would provide us with some sugar. Mom's friend Richard ate with us often and would contribute the vegetables, which he stole from a neighbor's garden.

One day, everyone rejected Mom's request. Nobody had any food to share. Even Shirley said she hadn't shopped yet, and Miss

Novella had no errands to run. All sources had dried up, and we had run out of food. That night, we went to bed hungry. The next morning, bright and early, Mom woke me up with an idea for a meal. She sent me with a large white dishpan to different yards looking for walnut trees in the neighborhood. I knew where a couple of nearby trees were, and people never seemed to mind if we took from them, so I began early in the morning before the beaming sun came out, climbing those trees and filling my mom's big, round, white dishpan with walnuts. It must have taken three or four hours to fill that pan. A neighbor saw me struggling with the weight of the pan and yelled out to me, "Hey, gal, won't you put that pan on your head, and hold it down on both sides to carry it. It'll be easier for you."

"Yes, sir, I'll do that," I replied, and I did. It was a cinch.

By the time I reached home, the usual gaggle of kids was already up and about playing hopscotch, stickball, war, and all our other favorite games. I was tired but wanted to join them. Mom knew what I was thinking and prophetically reminded me that we needed to get those walnuts shelled before dark or we wouldn't be able to see them since we had no electricity, then I could play. So, we got our tools together to begin shelling and picking the meat from the shells. Mom used the heel of her shoe to crack the nuts and the head of a safety pin to pick the meat out. I used a hairpin for mine. It was a tedious task. Rarely did a nut come out whole, and many of them were green, but we discarded none. When we were done, we had quite a supply of nuts to kill the hunger pangs that pushed and pulled at our guts. I ate so many of those half-ripened nuts that I ended up with a stomachache and couldn't sleep much that night, and Mom and I both had diarrhea.

Things didn't get better. Two days went by, and the only food we had was the near empty pan of nuts we'd eaten from two days earlier. By the third day, I was beginning to feel weak.

But God's plan kicked in. Mr. Harvey, a candy store owner we all knew, had died. Miss Sadie's daughter, Trish, and her nephew, Tank, and I attended the funeral. On the way back, we stopped at another candy store in Orlando, where they both purchased snow cones. I had no money, so they shared with me. We were in ninety-degree weather, so the ice felt good slipping down my throat and into my empty belly. I was still weak from hunger, and as we continued walking, I grew weaker. My mouth grew powdery and I began to feel dizzy. My blood sugar was dropping. I couldn't wait to get home. When I arrived, I told my mother how I was feeling. She suggested I lie down for a while but, being an active child, I refused to rest. I asked for permission to walk Trish home. Mom quickly said yes, especially since it may have been an opportunity for me to get some food.

I didn't get any food, but on my way back home, as I was taking a short cut by walking in a neighbor's yard where the wild honeysuckle grew, I bent down to pull a honeysuckle branch from the bunch and spotted a shiny quarter on the ground. I swooped it up with such vigor that I almost lost it in the bushes. With lightning speed, I got a second wind in my legs and took off running home, never stopping until I reached our front porch.

I burst through the door. "Ma, Ma, look what I found!"

Sharing my excitement, she said, "What?"

I opened my hand and revealed the shiny blessing.

She said, "Good girl."

I gave her a questioning look. "Ma, we can get some food with this quarter. Here, you take it."

My mom, being a wise woman, pondered for a moment and said, "Go to Mr. Fenton Bigg's store and get a big can of Gibbs Pork 'n' Beans."

I raced from the house with a renewed energy. I ran up the steps of the storefront and pulled the big screen door outward as I skipped into the store and up to the counter without any regard for my hunger pangs. "Can I have a big can of Gibbs Pork 'n' Beans, please?"

Mr. Fenton Biggs moved too slowly. Why couldn't he look at me and recognize my high. How could he not know the last time I had eaten? Didn't I look hungry? My peers always knew. I must have looked hungry after three days without food. Finally, he gave me the twenty-three-ounce can and took my quarter.

I skipped all the way back home with huge strides. Once there, Mom took the beans and used her old, rusty can opener, stabbing the top of the can and moving it swiftly back and forth to get the can open as quickly as she could. I could hardly wait! The old wood stove hadn't been fired up in a while since there was no food, so she just poured the beans onto a plastic plate. As I ate, she replenished the plate with the remaining beans until I had eaten the entire can without stopping or looking up. Then I licked the plate, remembering Mom's words. *"You never know when or where your next meal will come from..."*

But then I realized too late that Mom was probably hungry, too. I felt terrible because I had not considered her hunger. I hadn't eaten in three days. All I'd had was water and a few licks of the snow cone from earlier that day, so I didn't think of her when I should have. My little mind couldn't comprehend what she must have been experiencing. I apologized, but, of course, it was too late. She responded like a selfless, caring mother would. "That's all right, baby. Did you get enough to eat?"

I don't know how Mom found food for herself. I don't know if she had to wait another day, but I didn't see her eat anything that day. I've thought about that moment for years, and it sometimes elicits tears when I think of how I'd filled my belly and never thought once to say, "Mom, do you want some?" or "Mom, let's share." It's indelibly etched into my mind.

When the fourth day came around, we were back to square one. As a blanket of shade covered the sun, night crept up on us. The hunger pangs returned, and they wouldn't play nicely. This time, my head hurt, too. I lay on the side of the old, rickety bed and began to cry. I wanted to soothe the hunger, so I rocked back and forth on the edge of the bed until I drifted off to sleep earlier than usual.

Mom came into the room and woke me. "Phyllis, get up, honey. We going to get something to eat."

Those words jolted me out of my sleep. We left the house and walked through the familiar honeysuckle path to get to the street. Once on Charlotte Avenue, Mr. Thomas Rice appeared as if he had been waiting for us. He was our next-door neighbor, married to Miss Stella, and it was his garden from which we'd stolen vegetables when we were hungry.

As we walked down Charlotte Avenue toward Mr. Fenton Bigg's store, I overheard the conversation between my mom and Mr. Thomas Rice.

"I'll give you enough money so you can buy y'all some food. But you can't let Stella know," he said.

My mom said, "Why would I do that? Just come on, and let's get this over with. I hope you got a rubber."

Mr. Thomas Rice pointed to the store. "They got some in there."

I had heard some of the older kids at school talk about rubbers, so I wasn't completely unaware of what the conversation was about. I made the connection between the rubbers and the food. And despite how some people may have judged my mom for her decision, to me, it illustrated her strength and the love I knew she had for me.

We went to the store and came out with some bologna and bread. Before we got back home, it was gone because we needed to eat immediately. Once home, my mom made me go directly to bed. Then I heard the back door open and muffled voices in the air. I heard other faint noises, but I couldn't quite make them out. The next day, though, my mom got me up bright and early again and we walked what seemed like a mile or so to Be-Low's Supermarket, where we shopped for a substantial amount of food. I even got two of my lifelong wishes—my own box of cereal and a jar of peanut butter and jelly.

I never was that hungry again, but sometimes our plight still felt too dense to penetrate.

CHAPTER 13

A Future Teacher is Born

I was in third grade and back at Mary Estes Elementary School in South Suffolk or what was commonly called Pond Town. School was still important to me. I loved it and managed to keep my grades up, no matter which school I attended. But third grade was special because it was the first time I learned about the honor roll. Straightaway, I set out to earn the coveted title. I was self-motivated and didn't need anyone to prompt me. I looked forward to exercising my brain—it was one of the only things of which I truly had control. But this feat would not be without its challenges.

I was meticulous about my schoolwork, somewhat of a perfectionist, especially with homework and handwriting. One of the challenges was that I couldn't do homework that required a book because schoolbooks had to be purchased and we didn't have money for that. In fact, the only book in our house was a worn-out Bible. We didn't have electricity, so I had to do my work by kerosene lamp. This meant turning in assignments with soot on them because the lamp emitted black smoke, causing soot to settle on the paper. When I attempted to wipe it away, I unintentionally smeared the residue all over my work. It was a source of angst for me. I was a perfectionist, overly sensitive about the presentation of my school work, and I took pride in how it looked.

I submitted assignments on time because I had a deep desire for learning and following my teacher's instructions. As a result, I excelled in all my classes at each school. But it didn't stop my peers from ridiculing me. I was often the brunt of a barrage of ugly rants, mostly because, too often, I was dirty, hungry, raggedy, and generally unkempt. There was even laughing and bantering about my lunch. I only had ten cents a day and, with that, every day, I purchased a hotdog and a five-cents pack of Saltine crackers from Mr. Fenton Biggs's store. There was no place to cook the hotdog, and Mom was usually not home when I arrived for lunch because she was out finding work, so I ate it raw along with my crackers.

The kids had their own names for me, too: "po'ass," "hungry heifer," "high yellow," "red devil," "big red," or "dirty." I got the impression from some of their comments that they felt I didn't fit the mold of what they perceived a light-skinned person to be. In our neighborhood, most of the light-skinned people were better off than others. But I had the nerve to be light-skinned *and* poor. I didn't know what complexion I was. I simply saw myself as a poor little girl trying to survive during a cruel time. But they were angry about the unlikely combination, so they punished me for that unforgivable truth every chance they got, as if I somehow had control over my genetics or my economic status.

But all my teachers, even Miss Jones, simply adored me. At least they made me feel that way. Maybe they just felt sorry for me, but in so doing, they were the ones who built my self-esteem and helped me course through the time I spent with them.

It was late December of third grade and time to plan our Christmas party. Mrs. Mary Alice Davis, my third-grade teacher, asked me to remain after school. I thought she would ask me to help with decorations or something, but she had been paying attention. Instead, she asked if I had a quarter for the party. I dropped my head in shame and said, "No." I thought she was going to tell me I couldn't attend since I didn't have the money. To my surprise, she gave me twenty-five cents and told me to pay for the party when we came back to school the following day. I was elated. I thanked her and left, skipping all the way home in sheer giddy animation!

To make sure I wouldn't lose my treasure, the quarter was snuggly in my shoe for safe keeping. The next day, I felt a sense of pride when another student took down the names of all those who had paid to attend the party and my name was on the list. It was an exciting time. I was going to the Christmas party, and by December 20, I would also have a new baby sister.

Christmas vacation was on the horizon. I never considered getting presents for Christmas, but five days before the holiday, God gave me my little sister, whom my mother allowed me to name. She was beautiful, and I named her Cynthia Annette. I was nine years her senior, turning nine just six days after she was born. I told Mrs. Davis about my new sister and how Mom had allowed me to name her. She was thrilled for me, too.

On Christmas day, I got another Christmas present in the form of an unexpected delivery from Mrs. Davis. She'd bought twenty-four cans of Carnation milk for my baby sister. I had been attending school daily in freezing temperatures without a coat, so she also gave me a car coat and a box of assorted clothing. She gave us a box of food so Mom could prepare a delicious Christmas dinner. I had only asked for one thing for Christmas that year, to have the flat tire fixed on my bicycle that Mom's friend had purchased for me a year earlier. Mrs. Davis had arranged that, too. I guess she had spoken to Mom without my knowledge because on Christmas morning,

I had all the trimmings of a delectable meal, adequate clothing, a new baby sister, and one flat bicycle tire repaired! What a wonderful Christmas. My drooping hopes came alive again with the gift of generosity from Mrs. Davis. But not everything was for me. Other than the Carnation Milk from Mrs. Davis, Annette received another gift as well. Mom's long-time friend, Richard, gave us a crib that he had gotten from discarded items at a job he worked at for a white lady in town. The crib came at a good time, too, because our bed was getting more and more dangerous to sleep in, so I began sleeping in the crib, where I would remain until I was almost eleven. Our baby, Annette, slept with Mom.

Although I had escaped the wiry bed, I was forced to sleep in a fetal position because I was tall for nine and even taller by ten. The one advantage to sleeping in the crib was that the mattress was plastic, so I didn't have to worry so much about bedwetting.

Finally, Christmas was over. I had a good time. I couldn't wait to return to school to share my good fortune when it was time for our compositions about our Christmas vacation. When the time came, I eagerly awaited my time to shine. Mrs. Davis smiled at me and beckoned for me to come forward and face the class to share my composition. I stood proudly in front of my classmates and outlined every item, from the box of clothing, to every kind of food we had for dinner and my new and improved bicycle. But when I was done, as if it were her duty, the class bully reminded me of who I really was.

She said, "Sit your lying self down. You know y'all ain't have no food like that. You always hungry, and y'all is poor, so stop lying, you old red devil."

I was humiliated and felt defeated. I was telling my truth, but because of my circumstances, it appeared no one believed me. I stood there and openly wept. Mrs. Davis not only consoled me, but she addressed the situation with the entire class. She made this a teachable moment, asking us to close our eyes and think of a time when we had been made to feel humiliated. Of course, we didn't know what humiliation was, but it was Mrs. Davis's way to take liberties with the curriculum and teach us new words and new things, like the time we told her someone had written a bad word on the restroom wall. When she asked us what the word was, we all hesitated. Finally, I said it was "pussy," to which she responded, "Pussy has two meanings—it is a cat or part of the name of a flower, the pussy willow." Taking the mystique out of that word made us look forward to other opportunities like that. Learning the meaning of humiliation was one of those opportunities. After we were comfortable with an interpretation in terms we could comprehend, her explanation helped us understand that this kind of behavior was a result of trying to gain control over people, trying to frighten them for whatever reason to overcompensate for their own lack of confidence.

When we were in private, she spoke to me in that beautiful, sultry voice she had. "You may not have what some of the other children have, but they don't have what you have, either."

"What's that?" I asked.

"You're gifted. You're smart, and one day, you're going to be a school teacher just like me. Look at your beautiful penmanship. Think about how you get all your work done and receive nothing less than A's on everything. How about the way you help your classmates with their work? They don't all have that. And I don't want you to forget that you're special. You have a gift. Use it."

Those words remained with me. However, her words were never realized more clearly than during the summer of 2019, when Barbara Harris, my classmate and long-time friend of fifty years, shared with me why my classmates became the bane of my existence. She said, "Phyllis, you were smart, and all the teachers liked you. We were struggling with our reading, many of us below reading level, and there you were, in third and fourth grade, already reading on a seventh-grade level. That made the other kids mad and jealous. So they demonstrated those feelings by lashing out at you. And the class bully said, 'She ain't got no daddy, either.'"

Mrs. Davis was the most influential teacher in my life. I never forgot her. She made me understand that I had a spirit too bold to be broken and even at the tender age of nine, I vowed to never allow anyone to conquer it.

CHAPTER 14

He Dared to Darken Our Door

All thoughts of Jack, the man I believed to be my father, were met with dread and trepidation. I wondered if he would come home from prison and continue molesting me. And one night, we had that unexpected visitor—Jack Bivins. He had been released from prison and come to share Mom's bed, since he was still my mother's legal husband and thought I was his biological daughter.

His return was unwelcome. It brought back fresh memories of just two years earlier, when we were living with MinyNar. His unplanned return planted fear between each of my heartbeats. The moment I saw him, I remembered what he'd done to me, and the sight of him conjured up an unpleasant smell of sex that I would never forget. His presence carried an angst in me that I noticed even in my mother when she was forced to lay her eyes on him. My heart pounded in my chest like it was being beaten repeatedly by the swift swings of a hammer. It hurt. I wondered if this would be the beginning of another series of unsolicited sexual attention.

"Phyllis, this is your daddy. You remember him, right?" my mother said with apparent agitation. I think she kept up the ruse of Jack being my biological father because she was too afraid of the consequences if he found out I was carrying his name but wasn't his child. After all, he had demonstrated, on too many occasions, that she could and would be the subject of his violent rage.

Her demeanor easily made me feel edgy and encouraged me to fear him. I was glad to be sleeping in the crib, safeguarded from him while my mom slept with Annette in front of her. She was in the middle, with Jack at the back.

I was a sound sleeper. My mother used to joke that it would take a Mack truck to wake me. But one night, her moans and groans became that Mack truck. I lay still at first because I didn't know what was happening. What I heard wasn't pleasant to my ears. My mom's moans turned out to be faint cries that she was obviously muffling to shield my innocent ears from her pain. I knew the difference. It wasn't like the sounds I'd heard when I was younger and slept in the bed with the two of them while they made love. Back then, I would just turn over to the wall and suck my index and middle fingers to comfort myself while they had each other.

I attempted to turn over to see what was wrong. I tried to speak, but Mom said, "It's okay, Phyl."

Jack must've thought she was telling me something of which he disapproved because her next moan was a sudden shrill cry, as if someone or something had startled and hurt her at the same time. I ignored her whispered declaration that everything was okay and flipped over in the crib in a frenzy, raising my head in the dark room, straining to see.

"What's wrong?" I blurted out in a panting cry.

I was scared. I had heard of some of the awful acts of violence this man had inflicted on human beings. One time, at his mother's house, in the presence of his mother, nieces, nephews, several of his siblings, my mother, and me, he had gone into a rage when my mother complained about him staying out all night with another woman. He beat her unmercifully, as he had done many times before. No one raised a hand to intervene. During the altercation, he punched her in the head, and she fell against the dining room table, reopening a cut behind her ear that he had made during a previous fight. The cut began to bleed, and she was too weak to get up without assistance. I tried to help her. When she attempted to get up, he shoved me aside and straddled her, punching her again, this time, knocking her unconscious. To add insult to injury, he refused to allow anyone in or out of the house to seek or provide medical help for her.

When I turned in the crib to face her, I saw that he had his big, long, right arm wrapped tightly around her body, so tightly that it was impossible for her to move. The little light peeking around the curtain illuminated something metal and shiny. Between his thumb and index finger was the tip of a metal blade from the cream-colored, rusty, old can opener we used. It pressed into her abdomen every time she breathed hard. I didn't know what to do or say. I wanted to climb out of that crib and help my mother, but we had no electricity, only an old kerosene lamp in the living room with a smoky, cracked globe, an almost burned out wick, and little kerosene. Mostly darkness enfolded the room, with only the faint light of outside sneaking in past the curtain, making it impossible for me to see her eyes. If only I could see them, maybe I could know what she wanted me to do to help her. But I saw only the tip of the blade that tortured her.

That opener became an unlikely heirloom fixed forever in my mind. I found it amongst her things one day after she passed away. And to this day, it is still with me. I didn't know then, but my mom was being held captive. Her estranged husband had come back from prison to taunt us, insisting that he had a right to joint custody of his child, but my mother fought long and hard to keep that from happening.

Two years later, I learned that Jack wasn't my biological father and learned who my real father was by accident when I was twelve years old. One day, as I woke up from a summer nap, I overheard Mom telling a friend of hers that Jack Bivins wasn't my biological father; rather, my dad was Ernest Stevenson. I sat up in the bed, and Mom realized I had overheard her conversation. I was ecstatic to hear the news because Mr. Ernest had been in my life for quite some time and had always been extra nice to me. That was also why Mom fought so hard to keep me. However, it would be years later before I referred to my biological father as "Daddy."

I drifted back to sleep. I must have been sleeping fitfully because I woke up again twisting and turning. When my eyes popped open, I immediately looked over my shoulder to see if my mother was still next to me in her bed, but I saw only an empty space. I climbed from the crib, clad only in shorts. My chest was bare, causing me to shiver from the morning chill because the sun had not yet met our side of the street with a breath of heat. It was a Friday morning, late summer, so the stove hadn't been fired up. My feet were bare, too. The floorboards creaked as I strolled toward the front room. There sat my mother and Jack next to each other, engaged in conversation.

Now that I was up, Mom put Annette in the crib while she conversed with Jack. The discussion was not pleasant, and the grimace on Mom's face said so. I was invited in, and Mom instructed me to sit down. I did. She asked me if I wanted to live with him. In my mind, I immediately responded, *No!* but I was too frightened to verbalize my thoughts and wondered what would happen if I said no directly to him. I hesitated. Then I took the plunge and said, "No! I want to stay with you, Ma. Don't make me go with him."

She said, "Okay."

The sun was up, blessing the house with natural heat. Although there was no indoor plumbing, there was a pump outside and cold water ran from it, even on early summer mornings. I followed my ritual of pulling out the old, round white and black enamel basin with a small leak and chipped pieces of paint. The stove hadn't been fired up yet because Mom hadn't had time to go out to get wood from the backyard, and she was afraid that if she left me alone with Jack, he would run off with me. So I had to wash up with cold water in the basin. I grabbed my rag from the nail on the wall next to the sink where the basin rested and washed up in the kitchen. When I was done, I was ready to race from the house to play with all the children who were already outside frolicking around. I could hear them from the open window in the living room. The sounds were music to my ears because it meant removing myself from a grim situation inside the house. I got dressed and ran through the living room to the door.

My mother stopped me, and I knew what that meant. I needed permission to go out, so I turned and asked in a hurried voice, "Ma, can I go outside to play?"

"Yeah, go ahead," she said, smiling as if she welcomed my innocence as well as my obedience. "You know not to go too far."

When I was almost out the front door, I turned and yelled back, "Kay" and was off. Once outside, I engaged in the games the kids had already started. We played jump rope, hide 'n' seek, red light green light, Simon says, jacks, the limber rock, stickball, racing, mommy and daddy, store, house, post office, pick up sticks, and my favorite, shooting marbles. It was a typical boys' game, but I played and played well. I won quite a bit, too. I had a dishpan filled with marbles I had won from the boys. We engaged in a serious game of jacks. I felt especially lucky because I had on my lucky dress, my *only* dress. It was lucky, I guess, because it was the first new dress I could remember having. It was pale green, cotton with mint green plaid and stripes and a wide matching mint green cummerbund around the midsection, with two buttons on either side, one under the other. It was a dress left over from some of the things I had acquired from my short stay with Aunt Clementine and Uncle Lescell.

The day went on and we played hard. Lunchtime was uneventful because playtime during the summer was too important for food. A quick favorite sandwich with mayonnaise and bread or the infamous mayonnaise and banana sandwich was all we had. By early evening, a while yet before dinnertime, I decided to accessorize my favorite dress by putting on earrings. I didn't have real earrings, but the girls were of the habit of capturing lightning bugs and relieving them of the light from their lower abdomen and using the sticky residue from the disconnected light to keep them in place on our ears until the yellow glow died out. Then we would do it all over again.

In the mist of our last hurrah for the day, Jack emerged from the house. He approached me. "Come on. You goin' wit' me," he commanded.

"For what? What did Ma say?" I asked as he pulled me with him.

I struggled to maintain my footing, but it wasn't working. I kept pulling from him but to no avail. My struggle was futile. I didn't want to go, and I tried my best not to. He pulled me quickly, and his large, overpowering hands were too much for me. Sweat ran down my face. I was nervous and scared. This wasn't right. My stomach cramped. I had trouble controlling my bodily functions. My mind raced. I had to concentrate on not going to the bathroom on myself as well as trying to figure out where my mom was. Where was she? Had he done something to her? Was she in the house hurt? Was that why I was being taken so abruptly? Where was I going? What was going to happen to me? Was he going to take me somewhere and hurt my vagina again like he used to do? Jack's rude behavior, his silence, and his history of violence frightened me plenty, and I had no idea what was to come.

Mom, Geneva Bivins (1966-1970)

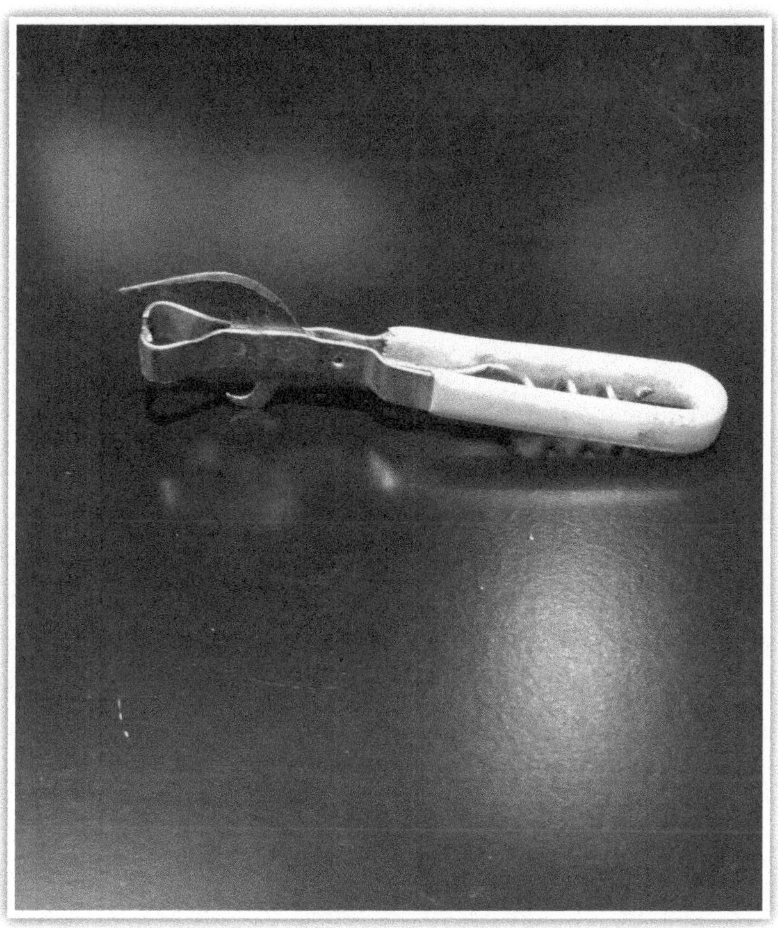

The can opener used to open the can of pork 'n' beans and the weapon Jack used to terrorize Mom (circa 1960)

CHAPTER 15

Further Acts of Injustices

As we left Pond Town, walking through the bushes and shortcuts from South Suffolk, we finally came out on the other side of town on North Carolina Highway. I was so scared and sick for my mother that I thought I'd begun hallucinating. I thought I heard her sweet voice calling me. But the voice I heard wasn't part of a hallucination; she was actually calling me. She had gone outside to call me in, and one of the children who had seen what happened must've told her how I was forced to leave with the man who had come from inside her house.

I could hear her frantic voice filled with fear and anxiety as she yelled, "Phyllissssss!" It sounded like she was calling my name in slow motion.

When I heard her again, I attempted to answer, "Huh!" But fear and tears were caught in the hollow part of my throat, closing it off, keeping me from being heard. My voice was too faint, like soft whispers running through a forest of trees, lost in the rustling sounds. I tried harder to pull the volume from the bottom of my gut, but I emitted nothing more than a whimper. Now, I was really scared. My mom's search for me made it clear that I was in trouble, that this trip was no ordinary one, but a kidnapping.

Her voice began to trail off in the distance. We walked in silence. I was tired. Where was he taking me? He continued to hold onto my wrist, as if he somehow knew that at my first opportunity, I would find my way back to my mother. I could no longer hear my mother's voice, and that made me even more frightened. It was getting dusky, and I wanted to go home. I wanted my mother. I was tired of walking because we had walked much too long. I cried inside and whimpered on the outside, but Jack never released my arm.

After walking for what seemed to be a very long time, we arrived at a familiar house in Saratoga, a house we used to visit by car because of its distance. It was owned by one of his family members. The house was a typical one for the neighborhood. A green and white awning hung over the front, branded with a large white initial. Matching metal chairs sat on the porch. One was a green and white metal porch swing with a starburst design made with round holes. There were too many plants on the porch and a rundown screen door with a fresh mosquito hole at the bottom of it.

We went in, and I immediately felt a sense of discomfort. Inside, there were four people at a folding table in the front room playing cards. On the table were cards, money, food, and corn liquor. The players were all loud. They were cussing, name calling, and enthralled in an intense game of bid whist. Other players sat around the table, waiting their turn to play. This was Lizzie Lee's house. It was Friday night, late summer, so everybody was getting their heads bad, drinking corn liquor, eating fish, chicken, or pig feet dinners, and preparing for the usual Friday-night fiascos. Just as we entered the room, Lizzie and her newest boyfriend—there seemed to be a new man in her life every time I saw her—got to arguing, and it escalated into a fight.

"I bid ..." The words oozed from Lizzie Lee's mouth as she politely placed her cards on the table.

"Heifer, what the hell is your dumb ass doing? Did you hear what I just said? You a stupid bitch," her boyfriend said.

"Who the hell you calling a stupid bitch, motherfucker? You can kiss my natural-born black ass!" She slightly raised her bottom from the steel-legged kitchen chair and half-lifted her dress, slapping her backside at him. But before she could reconnect with the chair, he was on her like white on rice, grabbing for her throat. He jerked her, trying to bring her down to the floor, but in the process, he slipped and fell. He tried to turn over as he fell so he wouldn't fall on his back, but he fell across the card table, which gave way, and he lost his footing, landing flat on the floor on his back. His head somehow got wedged between the front leg of the sofa and the end table, and he couldn't immediately get up. He was stuck. His feet and legs were partially sticking up in the air. Lizzie Lee loved it because he was right where she wanted him.

He yelled, "One a y'all get me the hell up!"

Everybody was so caught up in their laughter that they paid no attention to his commands, which made him even madder.

"What the hell is y'all sons of bitches findin' so damn funny? What, y'all see something funny?"

Lizzie seized the moment and began kicking and punching him, being certain to step back quickly between each blow, so he wouldn't be able to grab her leg and get the best of her.

He started regaining his composure. He got up and threatened everybody in the room. "I'm going home to get my pistol, and I'mma come back and kill all y'all no-good motherfuckers. Be here when I get back."

Nobody much noticed Jack and me as we went past. He practically dragged me into the house and called out to Lizzie Lee's boys to come downstairs. "Poochie, Head Power, Larry, Jelly Belly, y'all come on downstairs and get your cousin."

Five boys came down instead of four. Jack instructed them to take me upstairs with them and have fun. As it turned out, having fun meant locking the door and all five boys having their way with me. I tried to call for Lizzie Lee, but I knew she wouldn't hear me because she was busy with her card game. The boys wanted to shut me up, so they pushed me down on the bed and buried my face into the pillow. Each of them, ranging in age from ten to thirteen, climbed on top of me from behind and the front. They struggled with me, but finally removed my panties after they had successfully taken all the fight out of me. It had been a long day and night, and I was too young, too weak, and too tired to continue to fight, especially five boys who were much stronger and older than me. I continued to scream, but no one heard me because the pillow muffled the sound.

After what seemed like an eternity, there was a frantic knock on the door, and the knob turned and shook. The boys scrambled to get themselves together. I rose to see one of them pulling his pants up and another opening the window, tossing something out. Poochie opened the door, and Lizzie Lee and my mom came in. I ran over to her, pantiless and crying. My pretty mint green dress was still up far enough to show my bare backside.

My mother said, "Phyllis, where your panties?"

I felt guilty, as if I had done something wrong. "They had 'em," I said, pointing in a circular motion to all who were involved.

Of course, they all lied and said I threw my panties out the window and I had asked them to get on top of me.

I told my mom, "Jack told them to have fun with me, and they locked the door and did nasty to me from behind and in the front." But I didn't even care about what they had done. I was just glad to see my mom again.

She attempted to leave with me, but not without Jack putting up a fuss.

I prayed, "Please God, oh please, please, please, don't make me stay with him no more." I pleaded with my mother. "Ma, please don't leave me. Please, let me stay with you. Oh, please, Ma. I promise I'll be a good girl."

Lizzie Lee and all the people in the house felt sorry for me, and they all convinced Jack to let me go back with my mom. I still felt degraded by those who should have protected me. But I loved my mother extra hard that night. And even though she said I was never a bad girl, I tried to be an even better child to show my gratitude.

CHAPTER 16

"Say It Loud..."

Once back in Pond Town, I rested easier knowing I wouldn't have to be shared with Jack Bivins. But Pond Town had its own share of ugliness.

It was still summertime when I'd found a nickel while outside playing. Boy, was I glad! Money was a precious commodity. Having a bit of luck made my day. I held on tightly for fear of losing my nickel. With money came choices. I began to think about the possibilities. I could buy five cents worth of two-for-a-penny cookies or a mixture of two-for-a-penny cookies and kits, which yielded four or five pieces of candy per pack, or a large bag of popcorn, or a snowball. But my decision was made when the smell of Miss Lottie's fresh roasted peanuts punctuated the summer breeze. I had to have one of those five-cent bags of peanuts. So I hopped, skipped, and jumped all the way to Miss Lottie's Place. In route, I saw a friend, Rhudy, who lived around the corner from me with her mother and sister. Rhudy was about my age, a little bigger than me, with the most beautiful dark brown skin I had ever seen. But other children didn't see her that way. They teased her about her color and called her names.

When she saw me skipping past her house, she ran off her porch and began skipping with me.

"Where you going?" she asked.

"I found a nickel, and I'm going to buy me some peanuts from Miss Lottie's house," I replied.

"Okay. I'll go with you."

Once we arrived at Miss Lottie's Place, we did the usual to get her attention. Anyone making a purchase from Miss Lottie had to walk to the back of her house through an alleyway. At the back, her porch was screened in with a window space cut out toward the top for her customers. Inside was Miss Lottie's setup. There was a piece of furniture just under the screen opening and boxes of candy, chips, popcorn, cookies, sodas, peanuts, etc. all neatly crated so a potential customer could see what they wanted to purchase. To get her attention, we had to call her name loudly, so she would come see who was there.

"Miss Lottie!" we yelled with no immediate response. "Miss Lottie! I want to buy something."

We heard Miss Lottie moving slowly, dragging her feet to the back of the house. Her matted gray hair was always covered by an old, raggedy stocking cap, with a little ball knotted on top. Patches of gray hair popped out from underneath, where there were holes in the stocking cap. Once on the screened-in porch, she stood with one hand propped at the small of her back and her fingers pointing buttward.

"Heeeey!" she said in her southern drawl, dried snuff spittle in the creases and corners of her mouth. "What y'all want?" Her bottom lip poked out as Dixie Peach snuff showed a bit inside her lip. In her other hand was her usual spit cup.

"Miss Lottie, can I have a five-cent bag of peanuts, please?" I asked.

Miss Lottie strolled back near the door from which she had exited and slowly bent over a large burlap bag where she used a metal scooper to dole out a half scoop of hot roasted peanuts. She took a small, used brown paper bag, which had been refolded for future use, and snapped it against the wind to open, but because it was a used bag, she had to snap it again and again until it finally cooperated. She dropped the peanuts in the bag. When two or three fell to the floor, she methodically bent over to retrieve them and put them in the bag, too.

I wanted the transaction to end quickly because I wanted to eat my peanuts. The anticipation was overwhelming, but Miss Lottie took her time. When she finally brought the bag to the window opening in the screen, I handed her the nickel, and she folded the top of the bag and handed it to me. I immediately unfolded the bag and started chomping down on the delicious peanuts. I realized I hadn't offered any to Rhudy, so I extended her my bag. She took a few, and we both enjoyed them.

When she was done with her share, she asked if she could have more, and I obliged her. When she was done with those, she asked again and again. Finally, I said playfully, "Dang, Rhudy, you must be kin to the monkeys or something, 'cause you trying to eat up all my peanuts." I gave her more, and we continued up the street and to our respective houses on Hunter and Orange Streets.

Later that evening, Rhudy's mother came by to speak to my mom, and once she left, my mom called me inside. "Phyllis Bivins, you get in here right now!"

I knew when she called me by my full name, it meant something was terribly wrong. I couldn't imagine what because I hadn't done anything to anyone. Upon entering the house, my mother told me to go out back and get her a switch. "And don't get no little one, either!" Her final words were like a shot in the arm.

I immediately began to cry, not because I was guilty, but I wasn't a strong proponent of whippings. Many of my friends got whippings for committing the same infractions repeatedly. Not me. Once I was reprimanded for something, I never revisited that place again. But here I was preparing for a whipping for God only knew what. I returned to the house with the switch and knew what to expect; I just didn't know for what I was being whipped. I knew I would have to listen between cries and licks to her words to learn what I had supposedly done.

"Come over here!" She grabbed me by one arm as she began hitting me repeatedly with the switch. Her lecture ensued, each word punctuated by a staccato pause. "Don't-you-know-you-ain't-got-no-business-calling-nobody-black?"

I heard what she was saying, but I didn't understand. I hadn't called anyone black. I *did* know better than that. But she never allowed me an opportunity to respond or explain.

The beating continued. "That-girl-can't-help-if-she-dark! Who're-you-to-call-somebody-black-just-because-you-high-yellow? Don't-you-ever-call-nobody-black-again-as-long-as-you-live. If-you-do-I'll-send-your-hind-parts-away-to-a-reform-school-some-where. Do-you-hear-me?"

The switch fell to pieces, so she picked up her shoe and started hitting me with it. The beating continued until she was tired of hitting me, and her lecture ran out. When she was finally done, she asked me why I had called Rhudy black. I explained that I hadn't called Rhudy black and told her what I did say.

"Well, that ain't what Rhudy's mama said you said."

It was useless to continue the conversation because I was living during a time when an adult's words were law. If an adult said something, it wasn't questioned, even if they weren't forthright with the truth. Rhudy's mom hadn't told the truth. The reference I'd made to Rhudy about being related to monkeys was taken out of context. It was obviously how she saw herself. But the damage was done to both of us.

That whipping became inked onto my heart and mind. It wasn't until I heard James Brown instruct us to "Say it loud" that I felt comfortable enough to refer to myself or anyone else of my race as black. Even then, it felt awkward, especially if the other person was of a darker hue than me. I always remembered the lie, the beating, and the fact that, on that day, my self-esteem had been beaten out of me. I watched it lie on the floor and move slowly into a corner and vanish, where I wouldn't see it again until years later.

CHAPTER 17

Babysitting 101

Being ten years old is supposed to be a time of change and transition, challenges and delights, and thinking about the approach of adolescence. It is also a time when girls begin to navigate conflict and negotiate solutions.

It was 1964. We still didn't have electricity, only kerosene lamps, and we had moved again, this time, to a big two-story house, with no indoor plumbing and too many people. There were three adults and seven children, ranging from birth to age ten, and I was ten going on eleven. Lucille, her sister, Mary, and their five children shared two bedrooms, and Annette and I shared a bed with my mom. Lucille and Mary didn't mind the overcrowded living quarters because they had come from a large family. Including the two of them, their parents had a baker's dozen of children, and now those children had begun having their own children. As was customary in parts of the South, there were three or four generations living under one roof.

Mom was trying to improve our living situation, and while working at Suffolk Chicken Hatchery on North Carolina Highway, she'd met the two sisters. They shared Mom's sentiments about moving into better living quarters and were eager to go in together on renting a house. Lucille and Mary were glad to be emancipated from their parents' home and finally on their own with their five children. My mother, my sister, and I were just the opposite. We were accustomed to moving around quite a bit. Because we were so transient, no one place could be called home. But this new house was one of few opportunities we'd had to establish ourselves in a place we could call our own, at least temporarily.

My mother, Lucille, and Mary split the rent three ways. The house sat on the corner of Raleigh Avenue and Spruce Street. There was a fig tree in the yard on which we feasted when the fruit was in season. The house had a living room, kitchen, and an extra-long hallway downstairs, with three bedrooms upstairs. At the top of the stairs on the left was the bedroom facing Spruce Street. That was our room. There were two bedrooms across the hall. Those two rooms were for Lucille, Mary, and their five children. I was the oldest at ten. I had just turned ten in December of the preceding year and deemed old enough to become the live-in babysitter. Lucille, Mary, and my mother all worked varying shifts at the Chicken Hatchery, so during school hours, their work hours didn't much matter to me. They each cared for the children who weren't school age, depending on who was on which shift that week. However, I had to make sure I came home right after school because I had a key to the front door and was responsible for being home when the other children arrived, in the event Mom, Lucille, or Mary had to leave for an early shift. During the summer months, my sole responsibility was to be the caretaker to all six of the little ones when everyone else left dutifully for the Chicken Hatchery.

Having a live-in babysitter meant the women could work earlier shifts. This also meant they could remain at work to pick up an additional shift, which meant overtime and extra income for the house. I kept the six children from sunup till sundown. I arose in the morning and prepared breakfast for them when there was food. When there wasn't any food, I made up meals. My mom always tried to make sure there was money somewhere in the house for emergencies. It was usually less than a dollar.

Once, when we were all famished because we had played hard in the yard all day and worked up a tremendous appetite, I was expected to fix lunch for us, but there was no food. The children were all begging me for something to eat.

"Phyllis, I'm hungry!"

"Phyllis, my stomach hurts. I want some food!"

I remembered where the stash was and took the quarter from its hiding place, went to the store, purchased a seventeen-cents loaf of bread, and returned home to see what I could dream up. I took the little bit of sugar we had, dampened it with water to hold it together, and put it between two pieces of bread, feeding us all sugar sandwiches. The children said the sandwiches were good, and it kept them from complaining until one or all the adults arrived home and made dinner for everyone.

On another occasion, during my watch, the children all wanted to go to the corner store to purchase candy. Before the adults left for work that day, I had been given permission to walk the children to the store after all the chores had been done. We each made our penny candy and penny cookie purchases and obediently headed back to the house. Once inside, everyone enjoyed their own penny cookies and candy. Suddenly, I noticed Annette's face turning colors, and her eyes were rolling back and forth as if she were sleepy. I ran over to her and asked her what was wrong, but she couldn't say anything.

One of the other children said, "I think she swallowed that big red and yellow piece of candy."

I immediately grabbed her cheeks and forced her mouth open.

I looked inside, and right in the opening of her throat was the ball of candy. It was stuck and wouldn't move forward or go down. I hit her on the back repeatedly with the heel of my hand, but to no avail. Her body began wiggling frantically, and I didn't know what to do. So I quickly pried her mouth open again, inserted my index finger, and somehow managed to get my finger behind the ball of candy and push it forward, causing it to pop out of her mouth onto the floor. She gasped for air and began to cry. I gathered her in my arms, patting her on the back and soothingly told her to stop crying. Eventually, she laid her head on my shoulder and rested there in silence until she finally fell asleep.

Suddenly, I got a case of the jitters at the thought of what may have happened. My knees grew weak, and I sat. I didn't share with the other children how I was feeling because I didn't want to upset or frighten them. I somehow knew I needed to keep their trust in me for future situations. It would make it easier for me to handle them when I was in charge, and that was too often. To help keep everybody's mind off the incident, I did what I did best with them—played school. I was the teacher, and they were my students. Everyone had to listen to me and do all the schoolwork I assigned them. They enjoyed the experience, and so did I. It gave me an opportunity to stay connected to school, even during the summer.

Although I was mature for my age, in some ways, I was just an average ten-year-old child. I was afraid of the dark and swore the Boogeyman would pounce on me once the lamp went out at night. The adults were always standing in a corner somewhere, waiting for one of us children to walk past so they could leap out and scare the daylights out of us. I usually had a difficult time falling asleep unless my mother was in bed with me or at least in the room. Otherwise, I would pull the covers over my head to hide myself from whatever was lurking in the dark. But nothing protected me from what happened in my bed.

Many nights, when everyone was asleep, including my mother, I was awakened by the shaking bed. In the middle of the night, the bed would start shaking and eventually wake me up. I always whispered my mother's name so whatever was in the room wouldn't hear me calling her. I told her the bed was shaking and asked if she felt it, too. But she never acknowledged it. She always told me to go back to sleep because I was imagining things.

But to this day, on occasion, my bed still shakes, and I still don't know why.

CHAPTER 18

Growing Pains

Fourth grade brought on a different kind of change. I was just beginning to show signs of puberty. My breasts were sprouting, I was outgrowing the little clothing I had, I required very little parental supervision, and I was trusted and expected to show good judgment in all things.

One day, when the sun was tucked away and the moon started unfolding onto the clouds, the adults in our house were up to no good, and that night, I would be their victim of a cruel joke that remains with me even now. I proceeded to do my nightly routine in preparation for bed. That meant doing homework under a dimly lit kerosene lamp and worrying that Mrs. Blizzard would complain about the smudges on my work. I completed everything and was ready for bed, but as I approached the staircase, I heard my mother call for me.

"Phyllis, come up here," she yelled.

"Okay, here I come."

"Come in here for a minute. And be careful with that lamp so you don't drop it."

"Okay, Ma."

I entered the bedroom, walking slowly so I wouldn't trip while carrying the lamp. I moved to set the lamp next to the one already in the dimly lit room. I was stunned when I saw not just my mother sitting on the side of her bed with a sideways smirk, but Lucille and Mary, too. They each stood by the foot of the bed with their arms folded, smiling slyly with ill intent blanketing their faces.

"Come on in," urged Mom.

I still wasn't sure what was to come, so I was an obedient child who responded to a mother's request. Then, without warning, the two sisters grabbed me, each on one side. I didn't know what was happening, but the smiles moved to conversation.

"Grab her, y'all," said Mom.

"Come on, girl. Get her, Lucille," Mary said.

Mary struggled to control me.

"Damn, she's strong. I can hardly hold her."

"Grab her and hold her," said my mother.

Bits and pieces of the conversation rushed past my ears as I tried desperately to escape the jaws of hell. Finally, my strength began to wane and I was overtaken by their power. Lucille grabbed me by the waist from behind with her forearm, bending me over backward. Mary picked up my feet and legs, and they pushed and tugged until they were successful at throwing me on the bed.

The two of them pinned me down, and I heard my mother say, "Hold her down. Pull her dress up."

She asked me, "You got hair on your thang yet?" as if I were expected to answer. Instead, I struggled to keep my secret.

I screamed and fought harder than I'd ever fought. "No, leave me alone! Stop! Ma, make 'em stop!"

But my rants were pointless. The one person who could protect me was part of this insanity. The invasion of privacy continued until, finally, my secret was revealed. I cried hysterically. I felt so violated. They held me down while my mother forced my dress up and pulled down my panties. She brought the lamp closer and held it down so they could all see what was supposed to be private, a time of discovery, of inquiry, mother-daughter bonding. Instead, it was a time of great humiliation, mistrust, embarrassment, and fear. They'd seen what was supposed to be mine.

They laughed raucously at the sprigs of newly sprouted pubic hair. When they were done, I cried some more. I relented and balled into a fetal position on the bed my mother, my sister, and I shared. I whimpered quietly, my heart soaked in anguish while lying in the dark, praying to God they would forget I was there and move on to another victim.

In the days to come, I thought about how that experience had made me feel. I lost sleep thinking of ways I might get them back, but I was too young, too inexperienced, and too preoccupied with fourth grade and the other pains of growing up poor. They, on the other hand, obviously never thought for a moment of the long-term effect their childish, albeit abusive behavior had on me. So I resolved myself to focusing on fourth grade and Mrs. Blizzard's class. I loved her because, like my other teachers, she took care of me in a special way. She taught us a little bit about everything, too. I was a good student and never had to be reminded to do what was expected of me. In fact, where school was concerned, I was considered an overachiever; Mrs. Blizzard, and Mrs. Davis before her, had said so. And I believed everything my teachers said before I began to think more abstractly.

One day in class, we had all returned from our 10:30 recess, scurrying in from outside to be in our places before the bell rang. Just as we thought class would begin, Mrs. Blizzard stood in front of the class and said, "Somebody forgot to wash their underarms this morning." A few of us began raising our arms and putting our noses near our armpits to see if it was one of us. Then she asked who it was. When no one took the bait, she began calling each student up, row by row, to the front of the room next to her. She asked them to raise their arms, and she took a quick whiff. When she got to my row, I became nervous because I didn't know if it were me or not. I knew we did not own deodorant, so I wore none. However, sitting just in front of me was Patricia Gilchrist, who should have been in sixth grade but was still in grade four with us.

Mrs. Blizzard said, "Patricia ..." But before she could finish the command, Patricia hurled a quick, "It's me, Miss Blizzard."

My heartbeat rested and I was relieved. After Patricia accepted the call, Mrs. Blizzard went on to lecture us about good hygiene and how we should make sure we wash every part of our bodies because we were growing girls and boys. She said, "If you don't have deodorant, use some baking soda or leave some soap under your arms." She also checked our teeth to see if they were clean and our fingernails, too.

I was glad when that conversation was done because Thanksgiving and Christmas were looming, and that meant our annual Christmas program discussion, which included assigning parts. I was eager to have that conversation, but we were interrupted by an announcement that caused Mrs. Blizzard to cry. At first, we weren't sure of what happened. I wasn't sure if she was disappointed because one of us hadn't put on deodorant or if it was something else. Then another teacher stopped at the door; she had been crying and looking sad, too. We were later told that President John F. Kennedy had been assassinated. The children didn't know him the way they did, so we didn't cry, but we were sad because Mrs. Blizzard was sad. And if something made her sad, that was reason enough for us.

We all spent the rest of the day in a state of solemnity. It was

Friday, and we went home with the weight of the news that seemed to make everyone sad, even parents and other people in the neighborhood. Then on Monday, when we returned to school, the day began with us revisiting the conversation about the Christmas program. After all the anxiety of waiting, I was met with disappointment when I learned the girls were assigned the role of singing Christmas songs and were required to dress in navy blue skirts and white blouses. I didn't have either. But Mrs. Blizzard knew, and like Mrs. Davis, she did not embarrass me. She asked me to remain after school one day during rehearsal. I did and she asked if I had the proper attire. When I told her no, she said I might be able to fit one of her daughter's skirts and blouses. The next day, she brought both to school for me and gave them to me privately. I felt extra special because I thought she might think of her daughter when I wore that skirt and blouse, especially since her daughter, a twin, was also named Phyllis. That kind act became the reason I often bought clothing for many of my students through the years. When I saw them being hesitant to participate in an event, I saw myself, and I approached them with the same dignity and respect I had received from Mrs. Blizzard.

Next year would be different, though. We would all experience our first male teacher—Mr. Downing. He taught fifth grade social studies. But he taught us more than social studies. We learned about being on time with assignments and following through with what we started. He ruled with a small tree branch that he kept on his desk. Anyone in class without homework was subject to his wrath and that branch. My friend Barbara and I were one of few who never experienced it. I knew punishment and wanted no parts of it, so I did homework when assigned and turned it in on time. However, I struggled with reading assignments for homework. We were expected to articulate our understanding of what we'd read, but I didn't have books; mom couldn't afford to buy them. Mr. Downing expected us to figure it out, and I did. I would go to a classmate's home and borrow a book to get the work done and avoid being whipped. Whippings scared me. In fact, I recall one day a boy in class asked to go to the restroom when Mr. Downing came near to collect his homework. Mr. Downing must have been suspicious because he told him no, and the boy shat right there in his seat. He was whipped then sent to clean himself up. When he returned, Mr. Downing inquired again about his homework. There were no excuses! He forced us to plan, organize, prioritize, and demonstrate our understanding. In spite of the way he handled us, some of us still learned a great deal because we were forced to engage in activities that expanded our knowledge base and we were not allowed to opt out. The experiences in his classroom helped me understand that teaching was serious business. However, my approach as a teacher would be vastly different because I felt that some students also needed to be shown compassion.

CHAPTER 19

A House of Cards

By the time I was twelve, homelessness had been visited upon me at least six times. I would become homeless twice more before we finally found a steady home. Against my twelve-year-old advice and inexperience, my mother met and married Lewis Johnson. He proposed to her shortly after dangling the niceties of a home in front of us. My mother confided in me, asking what I thought of the two of them getting married.

Without hesitation, I said, "No!" I asked her, "Haven't you been paying attention to how Lewis beats Miss Ruth? What makes you think once you marry him, he won't beat you, too?"

Miss Ruth was Lewis's first wife. But Mom appeared to have a blind spot in her memory, giving little thought to what I'd said about him and Miss Ruth or their marital status; she had another agenda.

"Yes," she said, "but he said he would never hit me. And besides, if we stay here, we can have a roof over our heads, food to eat, clothes to wear, and you won't have to keep changing schools or homes."

I didn't care about any of that if it meant she'd be beaten the way he used to beat Miss Ruth. But she insisted, and they went gallivanting off to North Carolina one weekend and returned as Mr. and Mrs. Lewis Johnson. However, I don't remember my mother ever changing her name. I wondered if they were legally married. I learned later that he never divorced Miss Ruth, but a common practice was for people to leave one state and go to another to marry, even if the marriage wasn't recognized in their state of residence.

By all means, he was the first real sign of normalcy in our lives, a mainstay that began after our tumultuous trek from Pond Town to 421 Roy Street. That address is etched into my mind for so many reasons, many of which are firsts. It was the first sign of stability in my life. I had a secure home, with three meals a day, decent clothing on my back, and two parents. It was the first semblance of a family unit, with Mom, whom I longed to be with more than life itself, my little sister, Annette, whom I adored, and my stepfather, whom I both feared and secretly tried to hate because he was such a cruel human being. It was the first attempt at any real order in my life because now there were rules of the house, good and bad. This was where I experienced my first job with compensation. And it was the first time I was a student of the same school district for a sustained, uninterrupted time period while living with my family, rather than temporary foster parents.

We had decent furniture in the house. Anything was better than what we had in Pond Town. We didn't have indoor plumbing, which was still common in many homes. In our outhouse, we still used brown paper bags and pages from the Sunday newspaper or *Hit Parade* magazine in lieu of toilet paper. Although there was a sink inside the kitchen, it was not equipped for running water, so the small pump on the back porch was our water source. It worked well, except during winter, when it froze. When it was washday, my mother woke me at about four a.m. I would ensure that the old washboard was in place and commence to pumping enough water for three large tubs—one for the washing, one for the rinsing, and one for bluing, which was the substance used in the rinse cycle to make white clothes appear whiter. But when that old pump froze in the winter, I had to thaw it by tying rags around it then lighting the rags and priming the pump until the water came cascading down like a cool waterfall. Next to the pump was the swill can, a large bucket that hung from a hook on the back corner of the house. It was used for holding kitchen waste, which developed into maggots that eventually went to our pigs. The filth stunk like a mixture of fecal matter and rancid food but was common for those of us who had to accumulate enough slop to feed the pigs. The backyard was filled with chickens, ducks, geese, cats, dogs, and our billy goat. We finally had our own garden, too. Mom enjoyed planting and caring for it, filling it with wonderful green and red fruits and vegetables, like watermelons, peppers, cabbage, collard greens, string beans, tomatoes, and okra. This was a far cry from the pitiful, hungry, homeless state we had found ourselves in too many times in the past.

But 421 Roy Street birthed several other vividly imbedded indignities between our start there in 1965 and my departure in 1970, just two months shy of my seventeenth birthday.

Mom was 5'5" and weighed between 120 and 125 pounds when she ate regularly. She had baby soft pecan brown skin and cottony mouse brown hair that she often wore pulled back from her face with one bobby pin on either side. Her four top front teeth were missing from a beating she'd sustained from Jack. And she had the kindest, most compassionate heart of anyone I have ever known.

Lewis, on the other hand, was about 5'10", with a stocky build and a large beak of a nose that hooked at the bridge and curved downward at the tip. He had huge Dumbo ears with bursting gray hairs. He had a face of granite, with a medium brown complexion and salt-and-pepper, closely cropped hair. His canine tooth had been replaced with a gold one, which was fashionable at the time. Often, he wore one of Mom's sanitary pads because he had a large, bleeding hernia that hung from his scrotum, bulging like a large sack that made him walk funny. His hands were huge, and his fingers looked like fat pork sausages. On his right foot, he had four toes, having lost one in a sawmill accident. My sister and I secretly laughed at it and called him "Old One Toe," our personal nickname for him when he did something crazy. And that was too often.

Lewis Johnson was the name he answered to. But we weren't sure if that was, in fact, his real name. He led us to believe his real name was Walter Channing. Why the name change? He told us that one night, in the secluded area of a beach in South Carolina (where he was born and raised as a Geechee), several men jumped him. They beat him with iron pipes and kicked and punched him. "I was pretty beaten up," he'd said. However, he vowed to get them back one by one, but he never got more than one of them. He said he went to the home of one of the men, who was with his wife and infant child. He immediately shot and killed the man for his role in the beating but also shot and killed the wife and baby because he wanted no witnesses. He fled South Carolina, changed his name, and never returned until many years later, under the assumed name Lewis Johnson.

Lewis was twenty-five years my mom's senior. When they met, she was thirty-one and he was fifty-six and still married to Miss Ruth. It was common knowledge that he was a wife beater, and he beat Miss Ruth often. Everyone in the neighborhood had either witnessed it or heard about it on many occasions. In fact, I had witnessed it once when we lived across the street from them before our eviction and relocation to Pond Town. Once, he even beat her because she'd questioned him about his relationship with my mom.

Miss Ruth and Lewis separated not long after that. She went

to live with their daughter, Adelaide, in Hartford, Connecticut and he and my mom became closer. We were still living in Pond Town and very poor, barely finding food at the time. So my mom was happy to get closer to Lewis because his wife had left him, and he'd moved to 421 Roy Street, where he invited us to move with him. It came with furniture, food, heat, a gas stove, and an opportunity for a new life. It was a typical four-room, one-family rental. In our living room was a piccolo, a sofa with a chair cover, a cream-colored coffee table, and plastic curtains. Each bedroom had only a bed, dresser, and a nail behind the door to hang clothing. The kitchen had a gas stove, a sink, refrigerator, deep freezer, and a table and four chairs. The kitchen and living room floors were linoleum, while the two-bedroom floors were bare, exposing the natural but splintered wood. There were more than enough roaches and mice, too. The most disgusting and unwelcome guests were the chinches.

Our walls were made of horizontal wooden strips, with small openings between each board. At night, as we slept, the chinches crawled from the openings and into my sister's and my bed. No matter who slept in that bed, I was the only one who awoke in the morning with big, red blotches and welts over my entire body, where I had been bitten repeatedly during the night. Mom would come in sometimes during the night to check on me and find them encircling my body from head to toe. When she awakened me, I would climb out of bed revealing several red spots from underneath and around me where some of the bugs had died after their fill or from Mom smashing them to get them away from me. Every night was a night of miserable sleeplessness, but they never touched my sister, who slept next to me. On occasion, Mom provided me with relief by allowing me to sleep in her bed for a couple of hours after Lewis left for work. It seemed the scent of my blood and warmth of my body was the right combination for the pests.

Lewis worked a steady job because he was all about the Benjamins. Everyone had to do his or her share to contribute to the household. I was no exception. The first job I took on was that of a twelve-year-old babysitter. Once I was home from school, I had to walk from South Suffolk to Pond Town before five in the evening and keep a family friend's five girls, ranging from one to five years old. Helen worked at Planters Peanuts Factory on Culloden Street in Uptown Suffolk, and she had to catch the bus to work before her shift began. There were different shifts, but the only one she could get was late night, which meant she had to work until three or four in the morning. I kept those girls for one dollar per night, five nights a week, until her shift changed. I fed them dinner, gave them a bath in a large, round galvanized tub, and put them to bed. Then I did my homework. When her shift finally changed, her hours didn't coincide with my school hours, so she had to make other arrangements. I was glad because it meant I could return to concentrating on my schoolwork.

I was still getting good grades in school and doing even better than usual because, now, I was in a more stable environment, even though there was always the threat of domestic violence. Yet, I went to school faithfully and, for the most part, stayed out of trouble, except on two occasions while in sixth and seventh grade.

My mom often said, "Sticks and stones may break my bones, but words will never harm me." However, I found out that some words were very harmful and left indelible scars. I wasn't a fighter, but I could hold my own. Mom warned me that fighting was only for defending myself or my honor, so I avoided confrontations as much as possible. But on two occasions, someone called me out of my name, calling me a "high-yellow bitch" and a "red bitch." These were the only two instances for which I was excluded from school for inappropriate behavior. The first time was in sixth grade. Dorothy

Lawrence and I were having words, and she resorted to name calling. When the words "yellow bitch" rolled from her tongue, they were met with an uppercut that left her sprawled across the grass during our 10:30 recess period. Someone intervened before it could go any further.

The second time was the following year, when we were all seventh graders. Just before the end of lunch, Wanda Holland called me a "red bitch." Quicker than she had finished, I leaped on her, and we began to fight, tearing up Mr. Enoch Copeland's history classroom. We fought long and hard. In the end, I received the brunt of the punishment for two reasons. Wanda had brazil-nut skin, and since my skin tone was more reddish, the perception was that I thought I was better than her, hence her justification for calling me red. But that wasn't the issue at all. No one cared to understand the abuse light-skinned people sometimes received from their own. No one understood how it made me feel to be called red or yellow. It represented exclusion from everyone else. It made me feel like an outsider with my own people. And because no one understood, I was reprimanded instead of her. My punishment was to replace Wanda's earrings, since I had ripped one of them from her ear during the fight, leaving her earlobe a bloody mess. The problem wasn't so much that I had to replace the earrings, but a boy I liked named Larry Parker had given me a pair of earrings as a Christmas present, and my mom instructed me to give them to Wanda to replace hers. That hurt!

Getting into trouble at school was not a pleasant experience, and it didn't become a practice. There was too much at stake. Education was too important, and I had done well so far. I didn't want to start becoming a part of my own problem. And my seventh-grade teachers were important because they were the last stop before high school. They all played a role in my achievements, but two stood out—Mr.

Copeland and Mrs. Bennett. Mr. Copeland taught history as if it were a story told in lecture style, a new way of learning for us. I took it all in to prepare myself for high school. Mom said finishing high school was the prize. She knew nothing beyond that, and I hadn't begun exploring other possibilities yet. Learning under Mr. Copeland's tutelage was inspiring because he made me feel like I was being prepared for something better. On the other hand, Mrs. Susie Bennett was more than a teacher. She knew her craft, which was English, but she also knew when it was necessary to look at the social and emotional needs of her students. Once, when we were homeless again, before moving to Roy Street with my stepfather, Mrs. Bennett took me into her home for a short time. Another time, I came into her classroom after recess and proudly sat among my peers wearing red lipstick and eyeliner, which I had gotten from another student. Mrs. Bennett wasted no time sending me to the restroom to wash my face. She lectured me about growing up too fast and reminded me that as long as I was a student in her class, I would be expected to behave like a seventh grader. She said, "You have plenty of time to be grown. And right now, you are too young to wear makeup, especially red lipstick. Now take it off, and don't let me see you with any makeup again."

Her lessons stayed with me throughout my own teaching career. But however helpful my teachers were, and no matter what I did in school, nothing compared to what went on in our household.

CHAPTER 20

Everything Comes with a Price

In the dead of night, Lewis's wife, Miss Ruth, returned to Suffolk from Connecticut. She found her way to our house looking for Lewis and my mom. It was late, around two or three o'clock in the morning. She banged on the door continuously, demanding that Lewis get up and let her in. He became increasingly agitated because he said she would wake up the neighborhood. He got out of his bed and opened the door to greet her. When she began berating him for what he and my mom had done, he commenced to beating her. According to Mom, at one point, he hit her with such a blow to the head that she thought Miss Ruth would collapse and die right there. She didn't. Miss Ruth left and made it as far as the New York Port Authority, where she collapsed, fell into a coma, and died a few days later at a New York hospital. The cause of death: blunt force trauma to the head. We knew he had caused her death, but we were not allowed to discuss the matter or ever mention it to anyone. After all, she hadn't died in Virginia. We settled on the theory that she was probably mugged somewhere in New York City.

I was learning too early that life wasn't easy, and everything had a price. Our house was filled with some difficult lessons for a young woman to grasp. Puberty had been generous with me, but it proved to be my greatest curse. Being built like a "brick shit house" at an early age was more of a burden than a blessing. It meant that sick, disrespectful, and perverted men and sometimes women surfaced at the oddest times. That revelation was realized early one Saturday morning in our kitchen. I was twelve and had already begun straightening my own hair the old-fashioned way. I had an old, broken piece of a mirror with part of the silver coating peeled off the back, revealing gaps where I couldn't see my reflection. That meant moving back and forth to keep myself positioned where I could see the hot comb when it was close to my head to avoid burning both my scalp and my hair. Because the mirror edge was jagged, I had to prop it up on the side of one of our empty beverage glasses (a mayonnaise jar). Both rested on the side of the kitchen sink. Next to the sink was the gas stove, on which I had placed the straightening comb so I could heat it to just the right temperature that would fry the Royal Crown hair dressing and straighten the curls out of my hair, only to try to put them back in with my improvised paper-bag hair rollers.

Hoss Miller moseyed on in, disturbing me for a twenty-five-cent shot of corn liquor. I moved the hot comb to the center of the stove so it wouldn't get too hot while I served him. He must've expected other perks with his drink. After pouring his liquor into the glass from the gallon jug, I slid it over to him and immediately put the comb back on the open flame. But when he should have been reaching for his purchase, he reached for me, grabbing the fullest part of one of my firm little breasts, cupping it in his oversized, scaly hands. In a flash, images of dirty, scary men and boys from past experiences appeared in my mind. Only this time, I didn't feel quite as helpless. In fact, his grotesque face helped me deliver a seething blow to that hand in the instance it took me to reflexively grab the black handle of the straightening comb, which was hotter than the hubs of hell. It landed smack dab on the back of his charred fingers. He pulled his hand away faster than a cat smacking its paw on an unsuspecting mouse. When the message finally reached his little brain sensors, taking longer than it should've since he wasn't the sharpest knife in the drawer, he spit an obscenity at me, crowning me bitch for the day. His epithet was intended to sting; instead, it floated into my ear with ease like the lines of the beautiful song, "Lovers Concerto" by The Toys. I had sung my song; I had made my mark—literally! He'd gotten the message *hot* and clear. But that wasn't the end of it.

Hoss Miller picked up his drink and slung it down his throat, making a face uglier than a mud fence, a countenance that had become permanent from many years of moonshine and late nights, not to mention the scars of being a black man living in the South. He stole one more glance at me with those demonic, bloodshot eyes as he took a big, leaping step from the kitchen, huffing and puffing, madder than a snake, leaving behind the stench of his body.

I waited for my fate at the kitchen sink like a cancer patient at the doctor's office waiting to hear how long I had left to live. I was nervous. I knew not to mess with Lewis's money and his livelihood as I'd been reminded when watching him pistol whip men who came up short when it was time to pay their weekly tab. No sooner than the front door slammed behind Hoss Miller, in stormed the raging bull. The steam oozed from his hurling insults and cuss words. His four-letter expletives snatched my crown away, and suddenly the word "bitch," didn't seem so satisfying. I'd never been cursed out with such force and fury. I was reduced to the size of a dust mite over a mere twenty-five cents. Never once did Lewis ask me what happened or why I'd reacted to Hoss Miller the way I had. All he saw was a loss of wages. I saw a helpless twelve-year-old with no one to speak for her.

I wouldn't allow Lewis to steal my thunder. I had put Hoss Miller in his place. After that, his future visits to our house were uneventful. I served him his drinks, he hurled them down his throat as usual, and no words were ever exchanged between us again. That was fine by me. I didn't want to engage in conversation with him, anyway. Mom told me Hoss Miller once said she needed to bring me down a button hole or two because I thought I was Miss High-and-Mighty, and somebody needed to knock me off my high horse. What he said was of no consequence to me because he always spoke without the benefit of intellect. But Lewis had struck fear into my heart because I knew what he was capable of. I was convinced he was a restless spirit from the pit of hell. He was conniving and evil, to say the least, and I didn't need to test him by messing with his money or his patrons.

Lewis wasted no time getting his ducks in a row. Hoss Miller and others like him had become regular patrons, solidifying the set-up of his illegal liquor sales for cash or a line of credit and a piccolo. The music helped to make a prosperous financial marriage, yielding a profitable subsidized income. Lewis was enterprising, but he was nothing more than a hustler. By trade, he was a construction worker but recognized that it was seasonal work at best because of weather constraints. Either it would be too hot in summer or too rainy or snowy in winter. So he had illegal business ventures that brought in revenue for the house. In addition to the illegal sale of corn liquor, he sold state liquor purchased from the ABC store in Uptown Suffolk on E. Washington Street and broke it down into twenty-five and fifty-cent drinks for a bigger profit.

After all the years of drinking hard moonshine and now having daily access while managing the sales, Mom was becoming an alcoholic and her health was affected. But she couldn't avoid being around it because she had to sell the product and keep the books. I'd heard her on more than one occasion say to her friends that the alcohol helped to drown her sorrows. I knew her sorrows and the sacrifices she had made for my sister and me to have stability in our lives. Her hard life made life more meaningful for me. I worried that she would become like many of the patrons who had to have that drink every day. Yet, according to Lewis, things were looking up. If it was a really good day, somebody would come in and purchase a gallon of corn liquor and contribute to the piccolo to listen to the latest tunes of Fontella Bass's "Rescue Me," Slim Harper's "Scratch My Back" or Percy Sledge's "When a Man Loves a Woman." The longer they hung around, the more money Lewis made.

That piccolo in the living room brought in revenue, too. When the agent visited to collect the money, a small percentage of the earnings based on the number of plays went to the house. Mom could have put some of those earnings aside for a rainy day; however, she added it to the other household income. That was one of the legal businesses Lewis had. To further add to the income of the house, we almost always had boarders living with us, male or female or, in one case, both. Six people sharing the same four rooms, with the same two bedrooms. If there was a woman in the house, she had to share the one full-sized bed with my sister and me. Usually, she just paid room and board. However, the first woman to board was a woman named Millie. She was a prostitute, using my bed to conduct her business, and part of the proceeds went to Lewis. She couldn't leave soon enough. She was bad news. She took a liking to one of my mother's brothers, and in his naïveté, he began dating her, not knowing the kind of woman she was. One day, I became angry because she not only conducted her business in my bed, but she put me out of our room and carried on while I was in another room of the house. I resented her because of the inconvenience and how she was treating my uncle, and I threatened to tell Uncle WT about her lewd profession. She foiled my plan by telling my mom and stepfather of my intentions. My mom beat the hell out of me. The beating was bad; however, it wasn't nearly as bad as what she made me do afterwards. My uncle came over for a visit just after I had been beaten. He found his way into the kitchen to say hello and realized I had been crying. He saw large bleeding welts on my legs. When he asked me what happened, my mom made me lie to him and say that I had been disrespectful to her by refusing to complete a chore she told me to do. That hurt more than the beating because I had never disrespected my mother in that way, and it hurt me to hear my uncle say he was disappointed in me for disrespecting her. Mom made it clear that if I told the truth, I would be beaten even worse once he left. My truth would be seen as an infringement on Lewis's profits, so I never told Uncle WT.

Years later, when I could have told him, I decided not to. I guess exposing Millie and hurting him was harder than I thought. I also didn't want to jeopardize the invitations my uncle extended to me when he took me to his house across town off Norfolk Road to S. Lloyd Street in Suffolk. He had no children and would pick me up on weekends in his 1957 yellow and black Chevy to stay with him. Lewis never put up an argument when I spent time with Uncle WT. I loved those times because I had my own bedroom, indoor plumbing, plenty to eat, television, and children in the neighborhood to pal around with.

But one weekend, while he was still with Millie, she convinced him to take her out on a date. While he was in his room preparing to go out for the night, Millie told me she needed to talk to me. I thought she would try to keep me quiet about her infidelity to my uncle. To my surprise, she sat me down and said, "We going out for the evening. If you want to have some fun while we gone, here, take this birth control pill, so you won't get no baby." I knew enough from schoolyard talk that one birth control pill would not prevent anyone from becoming pregnant. I didn't take the pill nor did I need to.

When my uncle finally broke up with her, she moved out but still came around our house because she kept trying to be friends with my mom. She only moved three houses from us, taking up with Mr. Johnnie Moore. He was a loner and didn't seem to mind that she was a prostitute. Being a small man, only about five feet tall with cocoa brown skin, he looked kind of funny to us kids because, as small as he was, he had a potbelly. He wore a police cap all the time, even when he was in the house. No one knew what his hair looked like. He drove a motorcycle, too. And he always did crazy, fancy footwork he called a dance whenever somebody came around. Without warning or provocation, he would get off his motorcycle, perform his dance, spin around, then stop and take a bow. Millie, on the other hand, was about 5'8" and thick. She had milk chocolate skin and a thin black mustache. She had no formal education and relied solely on her looks and her body to live a "good" life.

One evening, my mom sent me to their house to borrow some sugar. When I arrived, Mr. Johnnie Moore and Millie were both in the living room. He was sitting in his recliner, looking at television while Millie lay sideways on a twin-sized bed with her arm propping her head up so she could see the television, too. When I entered the house and announced what I wanted, he got up and went to the kitchen to get it. While he was getting the sugar, Millie patted the bed softly, motioning for me to have a seat. The only place to sit was on the side of the bed with her, so I did. But once there, she quickly pounced on me, pulling me down on the bed, rolling on top of me, and gyrating her body against mine. Mr. Johnnie Moore came back with the sugar, set it down then sat back in his chair and directed his attention on what Millie was trying to do, as if it were normal.

I pushed her and tried to make her stop. "Move, Miss Millie. Stop. I'm telling," I said.

But she continued. She tried to lift my dress but because I was underneath her and fighting, she couldn't manage to follow through with her intentions. The scene must have become boring to Mr. Johnnie Moore because he soon said, "Let her go, Millie," and Millie got up.

When I arose from the bed, I immediately tugged at my dress to make sure it was down, grabbed the sugar, and headed for the front door. As I turned to leave, she grabbed my backside, feeling on it until I reached the door. When I got to the door, she fell into the door hands first, pushing on it with both hands to prevent me from opening it. Then she started gyrating against me again, this time from behind. I turned to face her, thinking it would stop her, but it only made matters worse because now she had total access to me. She tried to kiss me as I desperately squirmed, spit, and pushed to get out of her grip. Finally, she let up, and I was able to open the door. I ran down the front steps and all the way home. Once inside, I handed my mom the sugar, almost shoving it into her, and went right to my room in a state of dishevelment. My mom never noticed that something was wrong, and I couldn't figure out why I was a target for pedophiles.

CHAPTER 21

More Boarders

I was glad Millie was gone and living with Mr. Johnnie Moore, but we had two other boarders, a woman named Eldora, whom we called Chicken—I adored her—and a man named Mr. William, whom I despised. Chicken was a nice woman and taught me lots of information I needed to know about growing up as a young woman. She was never married and was originally from White Plains, NY. I never did know what brought her to Suffolk, but it was my good fortune. We talked about me getting my period and how to properly care for myself. And she suggested remedies for the immobilizing menstrual cramps I experienced each month. The remedies never worked, but it was nice just talking to Chicken and learning about female things. Once, she told me about a name one of her relatives was given based on all the women who lived in their village, which was a tiny part of town designated for the black people in the area. The girl's name was "Idalanabetahasatina," pronounced: Ida-lana-beta-hassa-tine-a, which was a combination of Ida, Alana, Elizabeth, Hassana, and Ernestine. We had so much fun with that name and all the girly conversations we shared.

Chicken was pretty. Her mocha skin was as smooth as silk. She had stylish clothing, too. Wraparound skirts were fashionable, and she had several. Because of the way they were made, I could wear her wraparound skirts, even though Chicken was much bigger than me. She allowed me to borrow them whenever I asked. This made me feel good when going to school because I didn't have to wear the same thing over and over again.

She wore a black wig. It looked decent, but she was always scratching it right on the top, which caused it to shift from side to side. Because she shared a bed with my sister and me, we saw her take the wig off at night. Underneath, she wore a stocking cap. I suggested that if she didn't wear the stocking cap, maybe her head wouldn't itch so much. But I didn't know that underneath the stocking cap was a huge bald spot right on top of her head; she had female pattern baldness. I loved her, so I never laughed at her head. In fact, I often told her she was still pretty, even with the bald spot. In return for wearing her wraparound skirts, Chicken would ask me to scratch her bald spot at least twice a week. And I accommodated her. I hated doing it, though, because it was always filled with a combination of scabs and dandruff, which grossed me out and reminded me of Miss Lula Belle. Yet, I couldn't say no to Chicken.

Mr. William had moved in, too. It was the only time we had two boarders at once. We only had four rooms. However, Lewis was not going to allow an opportunity to make some extra money get past him. So my sister, Chicken, and I were moved out of our bedroom into the living room, where another full-sized bed was set up for us. The sofa and the coffee table were removed to make way for the bed. But the piccolo remained because it was still a source of income. We were told Mr. William should take our bedroom so he could have some privacy, as if three women didn't need privacy. He was a Vietnam War veteran and a hefty six-foot-tall, dark-brown-skinned man. Mr. William had been honorably discharged from the war because he'd lost a leg and had the first prosthetic limb I had ever seen up close. Lewis said he needed the privacy because he removed that leg every night, putting it back on again the next morning. Each day, he sat on one of our wooden chairs right inside the living room at the entranceway of the door leading from the living room to the kitchen. That way, he had easy access to both the kitchen and the living room. But Mr. William had a strange habit that he seemed to have only when I was around. Sometimes, if he had no intentions of going outside right away or if the weather was bad, he wouldn't put his leg on. On at least three occasions, he called me into the room as if he needed to get something that he couldn't reach because he didn't have his leg attached. The first time he called me, innocently enough, I went straightaway to see if I could help him out since my mom had told me about his leg and I should be nice to him by helping him out whenever he didn't have it on. But to my shock and dismay, when I walked into the room, there he sat in that damn chair exposing the largest, blackest, hardest, scariest penis I could've imagined. I was mortified. When I first saw it, my eyes became saucers. I didn't know what to do. I couldn't move. He must've known I was shocked because he started shaking it at me as if to say it was going to get me! I had never seen a man's penis. My heart was thumping. I wanted to run past him, but I was afraid he would grab me. I backed away and into what used to be my bedroom, where I slammed the door shut, standing there, panting and resting my body against the door in case he tried to get in.

But I remembered he didn't have his leg attached, so he wouldn't be able to get to me that quickly. I didn't want to take the chance that he might suddenly decide to put it on and come after me with that thing in his hand; after all, it was now his room, not mine. So I eased the door open and scurried quickly through the kitchen and out the back door. I ran around to the front of the house and sat on the porch, where I remained until my mom came home. Again, she suspected nothing and never questioned why I had left Mr. William in the house by himself.

One day, Mr. William tried that same lame ploy again. I didn't answer when he called, pretending I hadn't heard him. But the second time he did it, I told Chicken, and she and I hatched a plan. One day, when no one was home but Mr. William and me, sure enough, he called me into the room. By now, he was comfortably in his new bedroom, where he had all the privacy he needed. He expected me to come into the bedroom when he called, so I obliged. But when I walked in and saw that big, black thing again, I reached down next to him, grabbed his prosthetic leg, and ran with it. I pulled the door shut after I was clear of him. I knew he couldn't get around without the leg, so from outside the door, I told him I was going to hide his leg, leaving him to explain to my mom and Lewis why I had possession of it. I told him he wouldn't get it back unless he promised he would never expose himself to me again. Chicken told me to tell him that if he exposed himself to me again, I would remove his leg from the room every time and wouldn't give it back until I was sure he would behave himself.

It must've worked. I kept that leg hidden all day. When my mom and Lewis returned home, they checked in on him because he hadn't left the room. They thought he wasn't feeling well, so he let them believe that. When Chicken came in for the evening, I told her of the day's events, and we laughed heartily about the adventure.

She said, "Dang, girl, do you still have the leg?"

"Yes," I said, and she urged me to return it. I did, and Mom never found out about that, either. Best of all, Mr. William never misbehaved again. Soon after, he moved on, but, to my good fortune, Chicken remained with us for a while longer. Her presence helped buffer some of the beatings my mom received from Lewis. Lewis didn't like to expose that side of himself when outsiders were around. He always acted differently when we had company. And occasionally, we saw a side of him that put him in another light.

Sometimes, when my sister, Annette, or I got into trouble with Mom and she took out her old leather belt to discipline us, he wouldn't allow her to hit us in his presence. We'd cry and he would say, "Leave her alone. Don't hit her," and Mom would come up with an alternative punishment.

When I was twelve years old, and big for my age, Lewis and I had gone to the grocery store. On the way back, he asked, "Do you want to learn how to drive?" Of course, I said yes. So he pulled over on the side of the road on Cemetery Street, about four blocks from our house, got out of the car, and climbed in on the other side. Then he casually told me to get in and drive, as if I had experience. I had never driven a car before, so I nervously climbed into the driver's seat and wondered what I should do. I thought about what I had seen him and other drivers do and went for it.

I was doing fine until I approached a steep curve on Cemetery Street. Right in the middle of the curve to the right sat the Savage family's house. In the yard was one of my classmates, Roy Savage, who was eyeing me as I tried to take the curve. I didn't quite follow the curve as I should have and ended up in his yard, hitting him and penning him against his house.

Lewis yelled, "Hit the brakes!"

"You hit me. I'mma git you, girl!" Roy screamed.

Thankfully, he wasn't hurt because I managed to stop the car; it coasted a bit and merely tapped him and his house. I just sat there with both hands on the steering wheel, holding my heart on the tip of my tongue. Knowing my stepfather's temperament, I thought I was going to pass out from nerves and the backlash I would surely receive. I began slowly opening the door, believing this would be the last time I ever drove a car.

To my surprise, Lewis simply said, "Where you going? Git back in here and finish what you started. You can't stop now, 'cause if you do, you won't ever drive again because you'll be too scared."

His words put me at ease, and I closed the door, backed out of Miss Savage's yard, and continued on home. When we arrived home, Mom was sitting on the front porch, and she could hardly believe her eyes when I pulled into the driveway with Lewis on the passenger side. I was ecstatic and couldn't wait to tell her about my new adventure.

After I learned how to drive, whenever Lewis went to work, he always traveled with a work crew in a truck and left the car in the driveway. Mom never learned how to drive, so I became her driver whenever she needed to shop for food or run other errands. I had no license and was a couple of years away from being old enough for a learner's permit, but we had a rule: You don't need a license or learner's permit until you get caught—so don't get caught. And I never did.

CHAPTER 22

Give Me Back My Stuff

Soon, it was summertime and the first time I would travel to another state alone. I was twelve years old and summoned to be the babysitter for my stepsister's children while she was in the hospital giving birth to another baby. She already had three children, and this was number four.

I had already been accustomed to babysitting Annette, so when Lewis's daughter, Adelaide, proposed to my mother and Lewis that I come to Connecticut to be the babysitter for her three small children while her husband, Roscoe, worked during the evening and she went to the hospital to give birth to their fourth child, it wasn't a stretch. They immediately said yes. I was excited because I had never traveled alone and looked forward to going away for the summer to experience a new environment. I'd write letters to my friends while I was away and relish in the surprised looks I'd get upon my return because they missed me. But things didn't quite turn out that way.

I noticed how Adelaide's husband, Roscoe, always stared at me. It made me nervous because I was aware of my size. I was twelve, but I looked more like a fifteen-year-old. I was developed and had almost reached my 5'8" adult height. I was very shapely, with a firm bust, small waistline, round hips, and long legs—a body that was a curse.

Early one evening, when Adelaide was in the hospital, Roscoe woke up before it was time for him to prepare for work. He frightened me by grabbing me from behind unexpectedly. I jumped and pulled away.

He whispered, "Come on, I won't hurt you."

But I knew not to trust that because men had said that before, and they always lied.

He began rubbing himself against me, and I got scared. I didn't know what to do. He was bigger than me, and I didn't know how to fight him off. I kept pushing him away and trying to escape from his grip. He had me pinned against the wall and the sink in the kitchen.

"Let me go! Stop!" I screamed.

He began acting differently, and his voice changed. "Just let me put it in. You're being such a big baby. Don't you want to be a real woman? You never will as long as you continue to act like you're afraid of a little dick. How old are you now, anyway, thirteen? Well, you're a teenager now. That's old enough. And look at you. You have a body of a grown woman. Your body looks a lot like my wife's body. You're developed like a real woman, so why not act like a real woman."

I was glad to tell him he was wrong because I was only twelve, but it didn't matter. He acted as if I'd said nothing. I pleaded for him to stop. I told him it was wrong, and I was scared.

In a final attempt to sway him, I blurted, "Plus, it'll hurt because I'm a virgin." But those words seemed to mean nothing to him at all.

"Well, still a virgin. I can help you out, there. You don't want to go back to Virginia still a virgin, do you? After all, your friends will be talking about their first experience, and you'll be the only one who can say a real man broke you in. Come on. Let me make you a woman. I promise I won't hurt you. And I won't put it all the way in." He stepped back, forcing me to turn around and look at him. "See, it's not real big. Touch it. It won't hurt you. And it'll be good, too. I promise you. Come here."

He pulled me to him by my waist. I pulled away, but he pulled harder and held me close to his body, gyrating against me. Desperate, I yelled, "No! Stop! I'm telling!" But he reminded me that telling wouldn't be a good idea. Telling would mean he would be removed from his home, his children, and his wife. And if that happened, it would be my fault that his children would be left without a father. It would be my fault that Adelaide would no longer have a husband. And it would be my fault if he went to jail.

He told me he knew I wanted it because if I didn't, I wouldn't have come there, as if I had a choice. Already, I was hoping Adelaide wouldn't get pregnant again because if she did, it would mean I would have to return the next summer.

"Come on. You act like I'm going to bite or something. Let me show you what your stepsister feels. Let me show you how good I make her feel. I have her screaming, not because it hurts, but because she likes the way I make her feel. I can make you feel that way, too. Come on. Trust me. I promise I won't hurt you. Just let me put the head in."

"No! You're scaring me. Stop, please!"

"Oh, I know. You think you're going to get pregnant. Don't worry about that. I won't come in you. Come on now. I'm getting impatient."

He pushed and tugged at me until I was in the living room and fell back on an armchair. He sat on the small orange sofa with short, brown wooden legs, and I thought maybe it was finally over. Then, without warning, he leaped from the sofa, causing it to move backward. Before I could do anything, he was standing over me. His dark chocolate body began to sweat. I scooted down. My heart was beating so fast that he noticed my blouse heaving from fear.

His chest moved in and out, sweat dripping with each breath. I wondered what to do. Crying in the past never helped, but I had no other recourse. I couldn't hold back the tears. Tears flooded my eyes and face, staining my pale blue blouse. My matching blue bell-bottom pants were wet with tears, too. My belly heaved. I thought I was going to vomit. My insides tightened. I smelled my own sweat. It smelled like fear.

Roscoe just stood there staring at me. My tears stalled him for only a moment. He quickly composed himself and, once again, started hammering me with quick, impulsive remarks that made me uncomfortable and confused. He hurled names and insults so fast that I lost control of myself and began crying profusely, and he had no choice but to quiet me down for fear I would awaken the three small children who lay sleeping comfortably in their beds, probably dreaming of their mommy bringing home their next new baby brother or sister. He put his hand over my mouth. When I began writhing, twisting, turning, and crying uncontrollably, he convinced me that he'd stop. When he moved back, I believed him. I was relieved and breathed easily.

But it wasn't over. I disrobed and went to bed. Around midnight, when I was deep into my sleep, he came to me. I thought he was there to say he was on his way to work; instead, he put his hand over my mouth and forced me out of the bed I was sharing with one of his daughters. He led me into the living room, where he laid my small body on the tiny orange plastic sofa. He opened his robe and removed his underwear. I was panic stricken. He warned me not to scream or there would be trouble. I was subdued. I just lay crying softly, waiting to be taken. I wondered what it was going to be like. I wondered if it would hurt like I had heard some of the older girls say. I wondered if I would get pregnant. My mother told me if I even kissed a boy, I could get pregnant, so I was sure that the probability of getting pregnant by Roscoe was great. I waited and prayed silently to God that it would be over soon, that it wouldn't hurt too much and I wouldn't get pregnant. I prayed that Adelaide would somehow find out and call my mother and say she didn't want me to come back again because there had been an incident. On the other hand, I also knew that if Adelaide found out, I would somehow get the blame. After all, Roscoe was only a man, and it was a girl's fault if a man looked at her in a sexual way. At least that was what we had been taught.

He took his penis in his hand without a condom and straddled me. I lay motionless. I turned my head to the side and bit down on my nightshirt. I wanted to scream, but he insisted I keep quiet, and I didn't want to know what would happen if I didn't. So I resigned myself to the fact that this forbidden thing was inevitable. In my mind, I ran away to a faraway place, where no one could find me.

He lay his slender body on mine and began forcing himself into my sacred place. When it didn't happen immediately, he cursed several times as sweat beads popped up on his face. He tried again and again but was met with the same resistance from my tiny vaginal opening. He pushed and pushed as I squirmed until it seemed to move in. I flinched and moaned in pain, with tears streaming from the corners of my eyes. I could feel my eyes begin to swell from the crying. My body hurt from the pressure of his body on top of mine. The area between my legs ached like never before. I felt him moving up and down in a rhythmic motion, gaining speed with every breath. He went faster and faster, and it hurt more and more. I begged him to stop, but to no avail. Then he finally grew limp inside me, and he fell fitfully over my body. I was still crying. I wanted so much for him to move. I needed to go to the bathroom. I wondered why this was happening to me. I felt wet, sore, and in pain.

After what seemed to be a long time, he moved. He reached for his robe, never said another word, and left the room, headed straight to his bedroom. I didn't move right away for fear he'd return. When he didn't, I forced myself to get up. I went to the bathroom and discovered blood running down my legs. I bled for more than a half hour and stayed in the bathroom until it stopped. I sat on the commode and cried, rocking back and forth, wondering why this happened to me. I wished my mom could know. I wished there was someone with whom I could share this, someone who could stop it. I was a long way from home, so there was nobody. I didn't know anyone. I couldn't call my mom. What would I have said to her? So I sat in silence and pain and let the experience drift into my long-term memory bank, where other such horror stories were tucked away. I was somehow compelled to understand that I was no longer a child and had to learn how to navigate this trauma.

I began to develop a deep distrust and dislike for men. They all seemed to fall into one of four categories: perverted, abusive, liars, or a combination of the three. After that night, I prayed that nothing would get in the way of my stepsister's return from the hospital.

Roscoe didn't bother me again that summer. But there was the next summer and the next. Adelaide had babies every summer for three years, and I was selected to babysit the children. And each time, I shuddered at the sounds of his footsteps and trembled when hearing his voice because I knew he would come in the darkest hour of night to steal more of my innocence. Finally, when she had no more children, there was no need for me to visit anymore.

One day, I heard that Roscoe passed away from a brain tumor. I couldn't find it in my heart to feel sorry for the man who had raped me during three consecutive summers. I merely said, "That's something, isn't it?"

CHAPTER 23

Chicken and Dumplings Anyone?

After Miss Ruth's visit two years earlier, we noticed an increasingly disturbing change in Lewis's demeanor. He began having more frequent fits of violence. Once, when my mom was in bed all day, weakened by a loss of menstrual blood due to what would later be determined as the need for a radical hysterectomy, he arrived home from working on his construction job and went into a fit of rage when he learned that no food had been prepared for dinner. He went into the bedroom and grabbed her by her hair, pulling her out of bed and onto the floor. As she lay there helpless and doubled over in pain, he lifted his foot, and it came crashing down on the side of her face and head. He stomped her repeatedly, holding his foot down and twisting it like he was squishing a bug with his heavy, brogan work boots. He cursed her out with every twist of his foot.

I had been lying down as well, sent home from school because I, too, had my period, and I always had cramps so severe that I would faint. Almost every month, I ended up in the emergency room for some relief. That day, I had thrown up in the nurse's office at school (vomiting almost always gave me relief), and she called for my mom to pick me up. Because my mother couldn't get me, she telephoned a friend who picked me up from school and brought me home. Sleeping helped take away the focus on the pain. I thought if I slept awhile, I could get up and try to prepare something for dinner for my stepfather. But I was awakened by the sound of his cussing.

I rose from my bed and ran to their bedroom, standing in the doorway, crying as he beat her mercilessly. Desperate to do something, I blurted out, "I'll cook!" I was old enough to cook, and I had watched my mom in the kitchen enough times to be comfortable, even though I was only an eighth grader.

I didn't wait for an answer. I turned and went quickly to the kitchen, where I began to prepare a pot of River Rice, which was a staple for every dinnertime meal. I searched for whatever else I could find that I could prepare quickly. Once the rice was done, Lewis smacked the pan out of my hand when I attempted to move it from the stove to the table.

He went into another fit of anger and rants. "I ain't having no woman that's bleeding fixing no goddamn food for me. Where the hell you think this is? I don't eat food from no woman on the rag!" It was confusing because my mother was also on her cycle. It made no sense, but then, none of it made any sense.

I later learned that, according to him, women who were menstruating shouldn't cook because the blood would get into the food. I often wondered if he thought my mom somehow managed to only cook before her period started each month. It was a crazy notion, but he had plenty of them, and his ignorance was overwhelming and exhausting.

I cleaned up the mess he made and walked to my mother's room to try to help her. He beat her regularly. I sometimes felt bad that I wasn't born a male child so I could help her more. She was in such pain that she couldn't help herself up from the floor. I kneeled beside her, put her arm around my neck, and hoisted her up. When she finally got back into bed, her face was badly bruised and scratched. The print of his boot was branded into her cheek. Her eye was swollen, red, and bloodshot. She lay there bleeding and moaning from the pain of the beating and her menstrual condition. I was helpless because of the fear of what might happen to us if we tried to fight back.

There were plenty more violent incidents. One night, during the dead of winter, in about two feet of snow, Mom hit our bedroom door hard one time. "Phyllis, grab yo' sister. We got to go!" she commanded.

I had been in a deep sleep, so I was confused and moved slowly.

She came by once again and said, "Let's go!"

When Annette and I emerged from the room, I was in my bedclothes and a robe, with nothing on my feet. Annette was four, and I was thirteen. She was small and also dressed in her pajamas. I thought we would be in the front room or kitchen, but my mother ran to the front door and yelled, "Come on! Move it! Grab your sister. Pick her up! We got to go! Hurry up before Lewis comes back in the house."

I didn't know he had left, but I knew there was trouble. He had only gone to his car, which was pulled all the way up in the driveway toward the back of the house. Just as we ran from the porch, approached the front gate, and were in the street, I heard the familiar sound of his rifle clicking. Then he fired two shots. The three of us hauled ass on the snow-covered dirt road, barefoot and wearing only bedclothes, at three o'clock in the morning. The snow came almost up to my knees. My feet were frozen. They began to ache and so did my hands. Then came numbness. Mom took Annette from my arms. She noticed I had nothing on my feet, so she took off her slippers and gave them to me; she had on socks. Lewis had re-entered the house through the back door. We were halfway down the block by the time he reached the front doorway. "Y'all better go, you sons of bitches. Because if I catch you, I'm gonna beat yo' asses," he yelled.

We reached the corner and stopped in the middle of the intersection of Roy and Cemetery Streets, turning around frantically in circles. We weren't sure where to go, so we continued to walk aimlessly.

A car came by and stopped. It was him. "Y'all get in the car."

At first, my mom hesitated, looking down at me as I hopped from my left foot to the right because my feet were so cold and had started turning blue. The only solace was that we were now on the main street from our house, which was paved, so the snow had been mostly plowed away and wasn't as deep. Annette was shivering. Mom reluctantly pushed me toward the car and told me to get in. She followed, still holding my little sister in her arms. We went back home because it was cold, and we had no recourse.

My sister and I returned to our bed, but I never fell back asleep for the rest of that night, thinking if I remained awake, it would protect my mom from his wrath. But about an hour after we were all back home, I heard the loud sound of flesh connecting with flesh. My mom pleaded, "Lewis, stop hitting me in my head like that. Lewis, stop! Come on now, you hurting me." She was crying like a baby. But he kept hitting her until he tired out.

The beating and cussing went on through most of the night. At around six a.m., things settled down, and he began his usual routine of getting up and preparing for his work day. I wasn't sure how long he would be gone since there was snow on the ground and there would be no construction work until it cleared up. I lay still, waiting until he was out of the house before I started my day to avoid contact with him. He insisted on my sister and me calling him Daddy. I found it hard to call him Daddy and even harder to hold a conversation with him. I didn't want to talk to him. He both frightened and disgusted me.

One night, I was again awakened by my mom's screams while he beat her, as usual. I longed to help her but feared the repercussions of interfering.

Lewis was seething. "I'm sick of feeding them sons of bitches. All y'all motherfuckers can kiss my black ass and get the fuck out of my house."

I only wished we could leave. But where would we go? Suddenly, things quieted down. Once again, I didn't go back to sleep the remainder of the night because I was always afraid that if I fell asleep, I might be awakened the next morning to find my mom dead. If I remained awake, I would be alert and ready for anything that may happen. But all was quiet. Too quiet!

Then I heard a noise. We had mice, so I assumed it was a mouse sharing our leftover dinner. But something was odd about the movement. I lay in bed and listened in silence. Curiosity got the best of me, and I eased up from my bed and went to my bedroom door to have a peek. I peered out of my door through a long crack, and there he was, ripping open a white packet of something and sprinkling it into the long blue and white speckled roaster pan that was half-full of chicken and dumplings from our evening meal. I was about to dismiss what I'd seen until I saw him drop the empty packet between the gas stove and the wall. When he returned to bed, I snuck into the kitchen to have a look. I tweezed my thumb and forefinger between the wall and stove to retrieve the empty packet. The shocking words on the packet made me immediately throw it back into its place. I didn't sleep another wink the entire night; anxiety kept me awake. I could hardly wait for daybreak, when he would be up and out of the house. Then I could get to my mom to share what I learned.

As soon as he left the house, I ran to my mom's room to tell her before she went back to sleep.

"Ma, come here quick. I wanna show you something."

"Can it wait? I'm sleepy."

"No, Ma, it can't. Hurry up!"

As we approached the stove, I pointed to the chicken and dumplings. Then I said, "Notice anything?"

"No, should I?"

"That's what I mean. You can't notice anything, but there is something there. Look again."

"Phyllis, it's too early in the morning to play guessing games. What am I supposed to see?"

"I saw Daddy come in here last night and sprinkle something in the food."

"Girl, what you talking about?"

"Look!" I blurted, grabbing the packet from between the wall and stove. This is what I saw him put in our food. And I know he wanted us to eat it. See, I told you we should've left here a long time ago. He trying to kill us."

My mom snatched the packet from my hand. "Let me see that."

I gave it to her, and she and I read it together. The skull and bones caught our attention first then the large printed words: Rat Poison. We both looked at each other for a moment.

I said, "Ma, what we going to do?"

She was speechless. She finally said in a calm voice, "I don't know" as she dumped the food in the swill can. She thought that would later be her way of discussing the incident with Lewis if the pigs died.

Two days later, the swill can was full and, as usual, we took it from the hook on the back porch and fed its contents to the pigs. Mom's plan didn't quite work out. Although the pigs ate the swill, they didn't die. A couple of them became ill, but that was it. Their brief lethargy wasn't enough for my mom to pose an argument for our case. So she dropped the matter, and he never mentioned it. Lewis never questioned why we were still around, but he did inquire about the leftover dumplings. Mom simply said, "I forgot and left the food out all night and it spoiled, so I threw it out to the pigs." We continued life with Lewis, with one difference—I never ate anything else cooked in the house unless I cooked it or I'd seen it being cooked and could eat it immediately.

CHAPTER 24

One Dance: Out of My Price Range

I was a teenager now and beginning to want things that the average teen desired. I didn't get an allowance, so any money I received would have to come from my mom or employment. Lewis believed in everyone contributing to the house, so working was never a frowned upon topic. One of Mom's friends told us about the possibility of work at a restaurant on North Carolina Highway. I was recommended, so I worked as a short order cook, making twenty-four dollars a week. It ended up being a great venture. It was an after-school job, and I worked there until the end of the school year because summer meant going to Adelaide's house again to babysit her children while Roscoe worked and she went to the hospital to give birth to baby number six.

It was 1968. Dr. Martin Luther King, Jr. was assassinated in April. Unlike when President John F. Kennedy was assassinated when I was in fourth grade, this time, I did feel sad because I was older and somewhat comprehended what was happening around us. In fact, hearing the news over the air immediately sent shock waves through us and I cried.

I was fourteen, and Annette was five, preparing for first grade the following school year. She was a kindergarten dropout, since kindergarten wasn't mandatory. I took almost every dime of my money and put school clothing for her on layaway at B.D. Laderberg, a popular uptown department store on W. Washington Street. By the time school started in September of 1969, she had an entire wardrobe and was ready to start school life. I was proud of my contribution. She always felt like my baby, since I had been the one there for her during the dog days of summer while Mom worked in the fields from sunup until sundown or when Mom worked at the Chicken Hatchery or was on one of her drunken binges.

When that job was done, I had to find another means of earning money. I took to the fields. It was a short-lived adventure that lasted all of one day. Two of the girls in the neighborhood, Gin and Darlene, and I decided we wanted to purchase matching outfits from B.D. Laderberg. The ensemble came in three colors, and we each wanted ours to be the same, distinguishable only by the color. The A-line skirt came in blue, raspberry, and purple, each with a matching sleeveless, floral button down blouse. The flowers were the color of the skirt on a white background. We got up at pre-dawn, tied our heads up and dressed appropriately for the fields, with old clothing, long and cotton, that provided durability and protection from the scorching sun. The length protected our legs from the sun, and we wore a long-sleeve top to protect our arms. The white rag wrapped around our heads covered our hair. We headed for the old field hand bus that would pick us up. We slaved all day in the hot August cotton fields and made a buck or so each. My mom thought we were going to the fields to pick cucumbers. When she learned it was cotton, she was agitated and insulted. She fussed me out and told me if I ever did that again, she would break my back. She reminded me that she was not sending me to school to become a field worker, especially a cotton picker. I didn't understand right away but later learned that she and others were forced to pick cotton, and because of the negative connotation and the back-breaking work, we shouldn't do it out of respect for our ancestors. I apologized and never did it again.

I wasn't planning to do that type of work again, anyway. We had spent an entire day wearing a sack with a strap fastened to it. We were told to put the strap over our necks like a crossover purse. The sack was almost as long as we were tall. Its opening was breast level and the bottom nearly touched the ground. Once the bag was filled with cotton, we had to empty it into a receptacle. This went on all day, and when we were done, all we had each accumulated weighed just enough for about a buck each. The work was grueling. We spent most of that day bent over, resting only when we straightened our bodies to dump the gathered cotton. None of us had an interest in continuing.

Things began to change even more in our household. I was older and wanted to have more freedom. I needed to socialize more with my peers. I grew tired of being in the house, selling alcohol to disgusting men who never knew their place. So I started asking if I could hang out sometimes with friends. I was never granted such privileges and resented my situation. As a way of rebelling, I decided to run away from home.

The first time I ran away was only down to the corner house, where a neighbor, Miss Ruth Savage (no relation to Roy Savage's family) allowed me to spend the night with her and her daughter, Barbara Savage. She promised to take me back home the next day and smooth things over with my mom and stepfather. She also understood why I chose to leave that godforsaken house. She was well respected in the neighborhood, but there was nothing she could do, except hope her words carried the weight I needed to avoid Lewis's wrath. And they did. Whatever she said, my mom and stepfather heard and decided not to pursue the matter any further. I was surprised never to hear of the incident again. But I was still very much like the average high schooler and wanted to change my situation.

Lewis wouldn't allow any kind of socializing, unless it was done during school hours, at the school where he couldn't control the environment. However, he did control extracurricular activities. I wanted to be involved in some of the activities at school, like cheerleading or band. One day, during an outdoor physical education class, the band teacher approached me and said, "You have big, pretty legs and should try out to become a majorette."

It excited me because I did nothing to participate in school life, so I went home thrilled about the possibility. But I knew I couldn't be the one to introduce the idea, so I asked the band teacher if she would. She sent a note home with me followed by a phone call. As usual, Lewis said, "If it's something that happens after school or after dark, she can't be part of it." My renovated hopes had been dashed. That was that.

But in September 1968, I decided I was going to attend my first school party. It was an annual party that everyone talked about, the Sweetheart's Dance. It was my second year in high school (we began high school in eighth grade), and by the time February 1969 came around, I would be fifteen. I thought I should at least be able to go to a dance once a year. I was never in trouble at school or home. I did all my schoolwork and had no complaints from my teachers. I had a strategy. I began talking the dance up by first mentioning it in early September, when school began. That way, when the time came for the dance on February 14, there would be no surprises from my parents or me. I told my mother about it with as much fervor and excitement as I could muster. I planned the perfect outfit with her. I knew they wouldn't pay for it or the dance, so I thought that through, too. When the question came up, I told my mother I would save up for it. She asked how since I had no means of income. I said I would sacrifice my lunch money until I had enough money to pay for the ticket and my outfit. Lunch was twenty-five cents per day; the outfit was ten dollars; the ticket was three dollars. I missed a few lunches, giving them up from September to late January, but I reached my goal and had change to spare.

Finally, it was getting close to the time. I reminded Mom about the upcoming date, as I had done once or twice a month to keep the event fresh in her mind. She said she would ask Lewis. I didn't want to ask because I knew the answer. I thought she might be able to state my case more convincingly because she knew more about how to talk to him than I did. The verdict was probably no, but my mother knew how disappointed I would have been if I weren't allowed to go to the dance. So, against her better judgment, she said yes. I was even allowed to go with a boy. Larry Parker, the same boy who had bought me the earrings that later became Wanda Holland's property. Larry was our local paperboy, and he was gorgeous. Everyone loved Larry—adults, children, and his peers. Larry was nice, a total gentleman, and I liked him, too.

He came to my house to get me for the dance. I was so excited I could hardly contain myself. I was going to my first dance and with a boy! I had on my new outfit, which was unusual because most of my things were hand-me-downs. But not that night. I had sacrificed too many lunches to not look good. I wore an apple green A-line skirt, a white long-sleeve button down blouse, with a sateen apple green ascot adorned with red circles inside larger white circles the size of nickels. The ascot lay under a round-collared blouse tied once to make it hang down in front to resemble a short tie. The soft knot was held into place with a pearl tiepin that I still have to this day. I wore white window pane stockings and black stack heels. My earrings were a round pearl post to match the pearl tiepin. I thought I looked cute, and I felt good about myself. This was a new venture for me. It was a kind of coming out party because, until this point, no one had ever seen me after hours in a social setting.

We left to take the bus to John F. Kennedy High School on Norfolk Road. But no sooner than we reached the corner, my mother came off the porch to the front gate and yelled down the street for my attention. I knew what she would say, so I braced myself and asked Larry to please ignore her.

In the loudest voice she could find in the pit of her stomach, she yelled, "Phyllis, keep your drawers up and yo' dress down, you hear me?"

"Yes," I responded and continued walking.

By the time we arrived at the school, the party was just getting good. I went in and greeted everyone, and they were all surprised to see me. I rarely socialized with anyone and most people didn't want to socialize with me, anyway, especially boys because everyone was afraid of Lewis. However, Larry was an exception because everybody loved Larry. It didn't hurt that he was the only paperboy in the area. He was always respectful to everyone, and when he delivered the papers, he always had a kind word to say to neighbors. I had a great time. Larry and I danced fast, we slow dragged, we mingled, then we did it all over again.

Finally, the night was over, and it was time to go home. We arrived at my house a little before my midnight curfew, even though we had to walk back home since bus service ended early. As we approached my house, I had an immediate sick feeling in the pit of my stomach. The closer I got to the house, the more my curiosity was raised. The curiosity changed to concern. I could feel the blood in my body moving and my blood pressure rising. I was lightheaded and surging with anxiety, complete with the trimmings: edginess, nervousness, uncertainty, and apprehension. The closer I came, the more my heart palpitated, detecting a clear and imminent danger.

The lights were all on in the house. The front door was stretched wide open. We could see straight through the house from the front to the back, and Lewis's car was gone. I approached the gate with caution. I asked Larry to stay with me until I checked everything out. He did, remaining by my side. I'm sure he sensed my fear. He grabbed my hand and held it tightly. Together in silence, we moved to the inside of the fence and up to the steps of the front porch. We walked up with caution. One step into the living room sent my heartbeat into a frenzied, uncontrollable pump. I wanted to take it out of my chest and hide it, so I couldn't feel how badly it hurt. I wanted to stop my head from throbbing, too. I began to wane. I glanced to my left, and there on my mother's bedroom floor were the first blood drops. We looked further and decided to follow the pattern of blood that led us out to the back porch. My eyes welled up, causing the blood drops to expand from my blurred vision. My tears quickly washed away the fun we'd had. We continued, but the blood trail seemed to dissipate once we were down the back steps and on the ground. In silence, we searched for Mom. Then we heard a low, soft whimpering sound. We both stood still and looked toward the doghouse in the backyard. We thought the dog was making the sound, but just then, the dog came from the side of the house and stood next to me. Following the sound took us to the back of the dog house, where we found my mom crouched in a fetal position, crying and whimpering, rocking back and forth, with fresh blood and snot streaming down her nose. I knew what had happened and felt like my heart had been trampled when I lay eyes on her.

We immediately went to her. I tried to grab her, but before I could, Larry removed his jacket and put it around her because she was shivering. The top front of her dress was a pool of bright red. It was obvious to both of us what happened. She needed medical attention. Larry and I managed to get her in an upright position and walk her to the house. Once inside, I called an ambulance. They came for her, and Larry and I went with her to Obici Memorial Hospital. The diagnosis—a broken nose. That bastard, Lewis, had broken her nose because he had been clear that I was not to go to that dance, and if I did, she would pay the consequences. She never told me that. Instead, she'd risked her safety so I could do what fifteen-year-olds did. I thanked Larry for what he had done, kissed him on the cheek, vowing that night to never ask to go anywhere again. The cost was out of my price range.

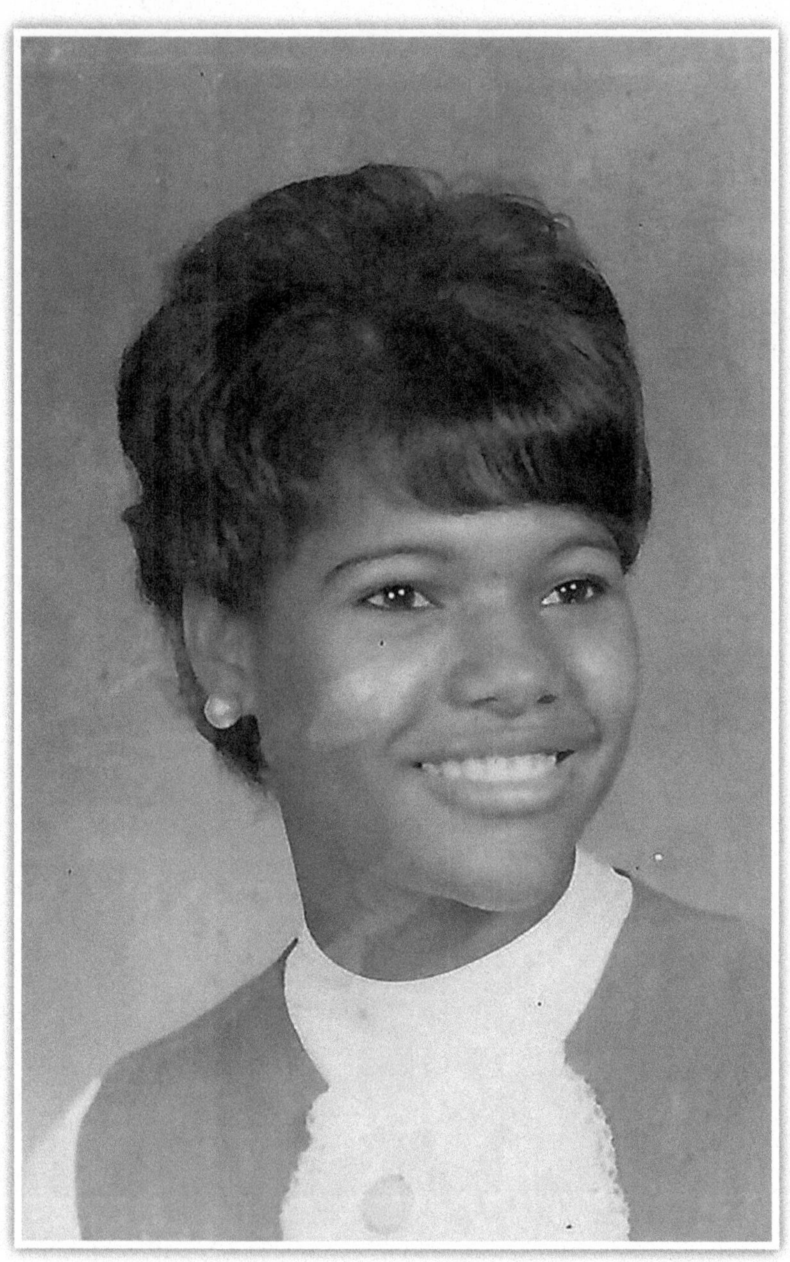

Phyllis, ninth grade (1968-1969)

JOHN F. KENNEDY
HIGH SCHOOL
Nansemond County
Suffolk, Virginia

Phyllis Bivins
TYPE NAME

1969 – 1970

Phyllis Bivins
SIGNATURE

Homeroom Teacher

Bus No.	Grade 10-3

REGULATIONS

1. This is your official high school identification. It should be carried at all times. Loss should be reported immediately to your homeroom teacher.
2. This card is non-transferrable. Cards become void if a student terminates his enrollment or is found guilty of transferring same. Card must be returned to homeroom teacher.

Phyllis, tenth grade (1969-1970)

CHAPTER 25

Death, Where Is Your Sting?

As time progressed and I grew a little older, the country was experiencing things I now fully understood. Year 1970 would see the death of Jimi Hendrix, the Vietnam War, which was still claiming innocent lives, and Diana Ross and the Supremes' farewell live concert performance in Vegas. One night in January, I broke my vow to never again ask for permission to socialize with my peers. It was a month after I turned sixteen, and I wanted to attend an after Christmas party at Lil' Bro's house. He was one of the cool young adults in our neighborhood who sometimes gave house parties. Usually, teenagers weren't allowed to attend, but this was considered a holiday party, and since he allowed his younger brother, who was my age, and my friend to attend, some of us were invited as well. Mom had been drinking heavily as usual and was passed out on the sofa. I managed to wake her long enough to ask for permission to go to the party. She said since it was in hollering distance and she could reach me if there was a problem with Lewis, it would be okay to go. So I did.

Since learning who my biological father was, I also learned that

I had two older sisters. By now, we had become more acquainted. Tina and Loretta were eleven months apart in age and were nine years my senior. They were both afforded a college education. Tina was a well-respected elementary schoolteacher, and Loretta was a housewife. Once Tina learned from her stepmother and our father that we were sisters, she often gave me some of her clothing. One dress she gave me that I absolutely loved was a long-sleeved, mustard colored, form-fitting, knit A-line dress. I had a nice figure, so it fit well. I wore it to the party with a gold-plated floral brooch with rhinestone pedals, black and gold shoes, and white pantyhose. The night was going well. I was enjoying this new kind of freedom while enfolded in the arms of my new boyfriend, Sonny, as we held each other close and danced to Diane Ross and the Supremes' latest tune, "Someday We'll Be Together."

My curfew was before midnight; however, at about ten that evening, we all heard several frightening thumps on the door. I had a bad feeling about that knock.

I heard Lil' Bro say, "Who is it?" after I had given him a signal to stall because my gut told me it would be my mom and Lewis.

I ran into Lil' Bro's bedroom and hid behind the door. They walked into the front room, where everybody kept dancing to James Brown's "Popcorn." Both my mom and Lewis said, "Where is Phyllis? We know she here." Lewis added, "And when y'all see her again, you'll see how she got her ass whipped. Tell her that."

Lil' Bro stood near the doorway. "We ain't seen her."

They decided to leave and look elsewhere, but they chose to exit through the back door, which meant passing Lil' Bro's bedroom. His door was open, and they were almost outside when my dog, King, stopped and began sniffing the corner of the bedroom door. Mom walked in, and there I was standing behind the door. I knew I would be beaten in the presence of all my friends, so I ran past her and Lewis like a bat out of hell. Lewis reached out to grab me but missed. My friend Brenda Lofton was on my trail, running because I ran. She was always down with me.

Lewis's vision wasn't good, and it was dark outside, so when he saw a figure on the railroad track, he yelled, "Stop or I'll shoot you in your motherfucking head right now."

But it was Brenda. She turned and saw the pistol aimed at her. Frantic, she yelled, "Wait! It's me, Mr. Lewis! It's Brenda. Please don't shoot!" She came closer so he could see that it was her. But I was there, too, just a few feet ahead of her on the tracks. When he saw the other figure on the tracks just ahead of Brenda, he cocked the .38 and ordered me to stop. I continued backing away from him.

He said, "If you think I'm playing, I'll show you." He raised the gun higher.

Then I heard Brenda screaming at me. "Phyllis, please come back! Please, please come back, or Mr. Lewis gonna shoot you, please!"

She was crying so hard, screaming so loudly and pleading desperately that I decided to come back. As I approached him, he allowed me to pass him, heading toward our house. Just as I was ahead of him, about five feet, I felt a hard blow to the back of my head. My knees buckled, and I went down like a wet dishrag in a pan of water, seeing colored stars.

Brenda ran to me and helped me up. I was bleeding from the back of the head. He had hit me with a 2x4 board. Then he smacked me across the front of my face with his oversized hand, sending me down again. This time, while getting up, I felt blood dripping from my nose and mouth. My lip ballooned, and the vision in my left eye was temporarily suspended. My mustard-colored knit dress was now two toned. Blood dripped down the center, creating a stream of big, red drops. Brenda left when I got up, and I staggered home, weak and dizzy. Once inside, I knew I'd have to face his wrath, and my mom wouldn't be able to help me. I went into my bedroom and sat on the side of the bed, contemplating. I easily cried about everything, but this time, I didn't shed one tear. I was hurt but angry. I couldn't believe this was happening.

Suddenly, my door flung open, and there he was. Mom was there, too, pleading for him to stop, but nothing could stop him unless God Himself came down and intervened. So I resigned myself to death that night. I rose from my bed while he beat me with his harsh words. I commenced to packing everything I had, which wasn't much.

With clenched teeth, he said, "Don't take not one stitch of clothes out of this house that I bought."

Surprising myself, I looked him straight in the eyes as I continued to pack my clothes, never breaking my stride. "Don't worry, I won't. The only thing you ever bought me was that green coat behind the door. It's still there if you want it. You can keep it."

Once I became a teenager, most of my clothes came from money I'd earned from odd jobs and errands or Miss Dorothy, my biological father's second wife, who gave me several dresses and skirts that belonged to Tina, my older sister. Miss Dorothy and my mom were good friends. She understood that whatever happened before she met my dad was in the past. Miss Dorothy had no biological children. Her job was to be my father's wife and raise my two sisters, a job she did very well. They had a reputation of being the distinguished Stevenson Girls from 109 Halifax Street.

Knowing I didn't depend on him for anything angered Lewis even more. He came closer and put his .38 caliber pistol to my head, cocking it, as if I were an intruder caught red handed breaking into his home.

He said, "Say one more thing smart to me, and I'll blow your fucking brains out right where you standin'."

I shifted my body slightly with a sense of resolve. I said to him in the gentlest voice I had ever heard from myself, "Go 'head. Shoot me. You can't kill me but once. So if you gonna do it, you better do it now, because I promise you this, you won't ever get this opportunity again."

God certainly had come down, and He was with me. I never understood where I'd conjured up the courage to be so brave, but my words somehow defused the situation. He removed the gun from my head and walked out of my room. My mom begged, pleaded, and cried for me to stay, but I continued packing.

My little sister, who was seven at the time, began tugging at my dress. "Don't leave me, Phyl. I won't have nobody to play with me or take me places," she said.

The truth was I never took her anywhere, except to places in the neighborhood like Lewis's convenience store when I worked there every day after school or Miss Louise's house, a neighbor across the street who provided a kind of refuge for different children on the short dirt road of our entrapment. But I was tired and not in the least bit thinking of playing with her or taking her places. However, I was concerned about her wellbeing in my absence. I had taken a beating for her once before because her little body couldn't handle it. If I left, who would be there for her when my mom got drunk and passed out on the sofa? Who would stop the unmerciful beatings she'd be subjected to? And who would prevent the eventual sexual advances and other unspeakable acts from those common bastards who frequented the house to spend their quarters for liquor during weekly visits? My heart softened. I decided to stay for then but not without a plan. I looked into my heart and found a place to begin planning an escape route that would eventually remove me from that wretched house.

That beating and near-death experience had changed the color of my thinking forever. I vowed that no man would ever beat me again. I meant that from the pit of my soul, even if it meant having to take a man's life. I had seen too much. I had experienced too much, and I wasn't willing to compromise my chance at a future. That was my first and last physical beating from Lewis or anyone else. Often, his berating—the name calling, the yelling, and screaming—felt worse than a beating. He continued to beat my mom, and every incident I witnessed was an affront to me. Each beating picked at a piece of my nerves and rendered me more and more afraid of men. My experiences taught me that if there was one beating, there was bound to be two, and three, and more. I made a personal commitment to my own welfare and to protect my future. After all, I was now in high school and needed to think more seriously about how to improve my station in life, beginning with finishing high school and possibly going to college. Mrs. Davis had told me I was special and had a gift. Standing up to Lewis that night was the first obvious manifestation of my gift. I had taken a step in the preservation of life—my life. I was beginning to learn quickly that my journey to womanhood would not be teeming with bright flowers and sun-lit skies, rather cracked vases filled with shame, despair, and misery. Now I had control of the reins and would have to make good use of that power.

I iced my face and went to bed, with Annette doing what she could to help. The next day, I couldn't go to school because the swelling hadn't gone down, and my eye was still bloodshot. A small cut was visibly open in the corner of my mouth. I looked terrible. Going to school would have been embarrassing and raised questions from school personnel, so Mom instructed me to stay home. I also made it a point to stay out of my father's view, too. Since I had learned

Ernest Stevenson was my father, we began to develop a beautiful father-daughter relationship, as much as we could without bringing attention to it. Lewis never suspected that Ernest was my father because we purposely kept it from him. We couldn't risk having Ernest and his wife banned from our house. My father, his wife, Miss Dorothy, my mom, and Lewis were good friends and socialized a great deal at our house because of the weekend party atmosphere. Their socializing made it easy for my dad to pay attention to me and engage in intimate conversations about how I was doing in school, what kinds of grades I was getting, if I was behaving myself, and who my friends were. He and Miss Dorothy visited most weekends. I was the youngest of his three daughters and quickly secured my place in his heart. I knew how much he loved me. I could feel it. Lewis never questioned it because it seemed to have unfolded organically. I didn't dare tell my dad about the beating for fear he'd retaliate, and that would mean trouble. I didn't want the burden of causing his demise or incarceration, so I kept the matter to myself. Mom advised against it, too.

CHAPTER 26

Life Is Expensive

Lewis's convenience store was right in our neighborhood, at the far end of Cemetery Street. It was a good idea because there was only one other store of its kind in the neighborhood, and it was blocks away. The winter weather had been especially difficult for construction workers, and work was sporadic at best. That winter kept Lewis home more than at work, a hardship for us in several ways. He was home too often, which meant we were more likely to be subjected to his fits of violence. When the money was short, he'd accuse us of eating too much or spending too much of his money—as if we had access to his finances. And his presence dictated control over everything, every movement, and everybody he was around. Even the daily patrons who'd stop by for a drink wouldn't tarry because his presence made them uncomfortable. But he was innovative, so he'd gathered enough capital to rent a small building that had once been used as a one-room shack located on Cemetery Street, the next block from our house. We could walk out our back door and be at the back door of the building in ninety seconds. He built a counter inside with several shelves and put in a freezer and refrigerator. There was also a small potbelly stove and a sink with running water. He included one small table with two chairs for those patrons who came in and wanted to linger long enough to eat their sandwiches and drink sodas or just chitchat with Mom on the days when she ran the business. When I was in charge, my friends came by to chitchat while drinking sodas and eating goodies. We'd listen to Jack Holmes or some other DJ from WRAP on the small transistor radio.

Securing that convenience store was the best investment he could've made toward my future. Mom generally worked in the store during the day. Since I had no life, when I arrived home from school, I got off the school bus and went directly to the store, where I worked every day, and since the store needed to be manned on Sundays also, I was told I couldn't go to church anymore. The store hours on Sunday kept it open until one o'clock in the afternoon. By then, the only church service in walking distance had ended for the day. My compensation for the work I did in the store was occasional permission to go "walking out," which meant I had no particular place to go, so I just walked around the neighborhood to see whatever there was to see. I was allowed to go walking out on Sundays after I closed the store, as long as I was back home before the streetlights came on.

Working in the store proved to be beneficial in several ways. It became a hangout for the neighborhood teenagers, so I got to socialize with my friends. It was an escape from the house of horrors. I openly courted my boyfriend, Sonny, because I wasn't allowed to have company, and the best advantage was my ability to put my plan of escape in motion by pilfering money from the empty gold, red, and blue King Edward cigar box every day. Lewis was so mean and cocky that he thought I wouldn't dare take money from the till for fear of his reprisals. But I was determined to make good on my promise. Never again would I allow a man to hit me.

The day after I was beaten and threatened, I took advantage of the opportunity and did some serious soul searching about my future in Virginia. I was responsible for opening and closing the store that day and counting the drawer. I did that for a few days to understand the daily average amount for the week. I was responsible for recording the varied amounts in the worn mini-spiral notebook that was kept in the bottom of the cigar box. Once I learned the expected average, each night, I skimmed between two and six dollars, depending on how successful the day or evening had been. I squirreled it away, not for a rainy day, but my sunshiny day; I had a plan to execute.

The average increased because my presence brought more revenue, since my friends came to visit me at the store daily, buying sodas, Vienna sausages, potted meat, cookies, chips, pickled pig feet, etc. They kept me alive. We talked, played gin rummy, and listened to the current tunes on the old black and silver transistor radio with a wire hanger antenna. It was a difficult time for me, and my friends helped me through it. They understood and knew how Lewis was.

Because of his reputation, we knew someone always had to be on the lookout for him. Someone would be positioned where we could watch the back door in case he was coming. However, the lookout person always made sure to be inconspicuously seated so as not to raise suspicion if he caught us off guard. When the lookout saw Lewis coming, he or she quickly gave a signal, and all but one or two of my friends scattered until he left, then they would return. Lewis didn't allow kids to hang out if they weren't spending money. They had been warned on a couple of occasions. "If you ain't buying nothin', you can't be in here. This ain't no hangout." When the lookout saw him coming from the back, some of the teens would run out the front door and squat beside the building until he left. If he came in through the front door, they would gingerly open the back screen door and ease out to the right and stand on the corner of the building until the coast was clear. The ones who remained in the store were the older boys who showed no fear of him and dared him to say anything to them. He must have sensed their bravery because there was never an exchange between them.

The first week after Lil' Bro's party, when my friends came to the store, I was embarrassed because my eye was still bloodshot and blackened and my lip was still swollen in the left corner. My face was puffy, too. Lewis's fingerprints were still imprinted on the side of my face like a reminder. But they all understood. They didn't laugh, and they knew how mean he was and didn't want to cause me any trouble, so they stayed out of his way.

My boyfriend, Sonny, was seven years my senior. I was sixteen and he was twenty-three. It felt good thinking someone cared about me, especially someone so much older. But that meant trouble. While Sonny was very gentle with me, he was also only pursuing a conquest—a young, attractive teenager who looked like a woman and was obviously vulnerable. I had very little experience with boyfriends and only negative encounters with men. My inexperience kept me from understanding how to manage a real relationship, and he took advantage of my naivete. Soon after I became involved with him, we became forever attached because I got pregnant. I wasn't aware of my pregnancy until I was four months along, since I continued to have a period.

Our relationship continued in secret. No boy or man dared come to my house because of Lewis's reputation. I also continued school. I was in the tenth grade. As was the practice, if someone reported a pregnancy or even suspected one, the girl was called to the nurse's office, evaluated, sent to her family physician, and given a doctor's note stating she was either pregnant or not. If it was determined that she was pregnant, she'd have to leave school and, in most cases, relocate. Those were the rules. In my case, the doctor's visit was just another traumatizing experience.

I had to make the visit alone because I didn't know if I was pregnant yet; therefore, I hadn't told Mom, and it was my first visit with a gynecologist. On the day of the visit, after the examination, the doctor said, "Phyllis, are you ready to be a mother?"

I asked, "What do you mean?"

"You are four months pregnant."

"But how could that happen? I haven't missed my period?" I was confused and sure he had made a mistake. But the bleeding I had been experiencing was not normal periods. It was just light, irregular bleeding.

A pregnancy would surely interfere with my plan. He asked me to get dressed and come into his office so he could talk to me about it. Once there, he said, "In order to stay at school and finish out this term, you will require a medical note from me, saying you are being sent back to school pending further test results and reevaluation, which will be done at a later date. This way, you'll be able to complete the school year because your baby won't be due until September fifteenth."

He arose from his desk and walked to the other side, where he grabbed my hand and led me to the front of his desk. The touch felt funny. He picked me up and sat me on the corner of the desk. My heart began misbehaving, reminding me of an old rerun from eight years earlier. I wondered if all men were the same as the ones who had mistreated me—heinous, pedophiles, or a combination of both.

He conversed with me about my condition. As we talked, he incorporated bits and pieces of conversation that had nothing to do with my pregnancy. He talked about how pretty I was, which made me want to cry because, somehow, being pretty was still my curse. As he continued to talk, he discussed in an almost professional manner how shapely my body was. As he unbuttoned my blouse and tugged at my bra, I kept trying to re-button my blouse, but he reminded me that I needed the note. Once my shirt was completely open, he lifted the left cup of my bra and leaned into me. I pulled back from him, and a single teardrop formed, dropping near his head. He explained that this was part of the examination. I had never seen a doctor before as a teenager and certainly not one for pregnancy. I assumed it was part of the routine to check my breast for milk. But his actions didn't seem appropriate. He held my firm breast in his hand and put his mouth on it, sucking with his eyes closed. My body revolted. I felt violated but didn't know how to express my feelings. I hated it. I hated him. I hated being pretty. I hated every compliment ever sent in my direction. I hated being a woman. I hated the way men behaved. My tears exploded, cascading down into his hair. He ignored my emotional state. I was finally convinced that there was something wrong with me because more than a half a dozen times, I'd found myself in situations where men or women thought it was okay to have their way with me.

He continued sucking for what seemed like thirty seconds or so. Then he stopped, moved away, and said, "There. I had to make sure there's milk in there. That didn't hurt, did it?"

My thinking had been twisted into indistinguishable little knots and I was confused. I replied with my head hung in shame. "No, it didn't hurt." But what did hurt was the bottom of my soul.

Robotically, I buttoned my emotions and my blouse and sat, waiting for further instructions. This was the first time anyone had ever had his mouth on my breasts, and the doctor made it feel dirty and shameful. For my cooperation, he provided me with a medical note and sent me on my way. Life was expensive, with hefty prices to be paid.

I returned to school with my note and handed it to the nurse, who accepted it with crossed eyes. I always thought she knew the note was just to buy time, but she never let on, and I completed the tenth grade wearing my usual clothing, with one exception—I also wore two girdles to help hide the secret.

Once I amassed enough nerve to share the news of my pregnancy with my mom, I wasn't sure how she would take it. Then there was the task of telling Lewis. The anxiety that came with having to tell him was almost unbearable, but I knew he would eventually find out.

Terrified, I finally told my mom with tears in my eyes and a lump in my throat. "Mom, I have something to tell you."

"What?"

I was numb. "I'm four months pregnant and will be having a baby in September."

To my surprise, she accepted the news as if I had made a store purchase and placed the items I'd bought on the counter for quick examination. I felt like she already suspected my pregnancy and the news was simply confirmation.

She said, "Well, we have to see what we gonna do about it."

I wondered what that meant. I wondered how I would approach the subject with Lewis, but as if reading my mind, Mom insisted, "I will handle this with Lewis."

I didn't know what to think of that. However, I let her address it with her husband out of fear. She did and, whatever his reaction was, it never affected me because not once did we speak about my pregnancy or the identity of the father.

My mom came into our convenience store one Sunday morning carrying a small brown paper bag. She went over to the sink and took out a small bottle and a glass. Then she ran water from the sink into the fifty-cents-sized corn liquor glass, stirred a mixture, and handed it to me. She said, "Drink this and chase it with this corn liquor. It ain't gonna hurt you none." She left out the back door with her head hung down and didn't say a word.

Her demeanor suggested she was asking me to do something against her better judgment. I knew I should avoid the concoction. And I did. I poured it and the liquor down the sink. When she returned hours later, inquiring about it, I said I had drunk it. I knew what the concoction was—quinine. By the next morning, when I hadn't aborted my baby, Mom thought it simply didn't work. I stayed out of Lewis's way as much as possible, trying desperately not to antagonize him. He rarely spoke to me and vice versa. I made it a point to leave a room if he entered, trying to be as invisible as possible.

I got through the remainder of the school year. I was five months pregnant when June came, and I spent the remainder of my pregnancy at home staying out of Lewis's way. I didn't return to school in September because I was already eight months pregnant and obviously too far along to return.

When I went into labor, I was scared, but Mom was there to help me through it. For the first time during my pregnancy, Lewis said something about it. "Is it time for her to go in?" he asked.

"Yeah," said Mom.

"I'll get the car started," he mumbled.

Sister, Annette (left) and Phyllis (1970)

CHAPTER 27

An Angel, a Devil and a Good Neighbor

On October 9, 1970, just two months shy of my seventeenth birthday, I delivered my first child. This was my first hospital stay. I had hoped it would be a pleasant one, since I was there to deliver my baby, not for an illness. However, that thought was banished once the hospital personnel began their "tour of duty," each nurse and doctor completing their rounds of shifts. First, there was an incident when initially meeting my child. I was told I'd had a baby girl, but the baby they brought to me was a boy. I protested, and they corrected the error.

Then I met her! She was awfully beautiful, with toast brown skin and little hands that I couldn't resist kissing and holding. She was so special, sweet, and precious. My mom immediately loved her and wanted a better life for her than we had, as I did. Mom called her Angel. I thought long and hard about what I would name her. I didn't recall ever hearing the names Twana or Latrice, so I chose those names. I had something that belonged to me. My own responsibility. And it would be up to me to ensure her survival and a childhood—something I lacked.

When it was time to let her go, I wanted to ask if she could remain with me. She was so sweet, and I thought her absence would bring me angst. I didn't want her to be given to another family by accident. I wondered if they would remember that she was mine. I prayed for clarity of mind for the women attending to our babies in that nursery.

The nurse asked who the father of my child was. But during a conversation with my mother and Sonny, we determined it was best to say I didn't know who the father was because it would cause problems since we weren't married. My lack of experience told me to follow the advice.

"I don't know," I responded.

They marked the birth certificate "father unknown."

I was then asked to give the correct spelling of my baby's name. I complied, carefully spelling T-w-a-n-a L-a-t-r-i-c-e B-i-v-i-n-s. Yet when I received my daughter's birth certificate, it read Tawana Latrice Bivins. I inquired about the incorrect spelling of her first name, and the nurse told me it was the correct way to spell Tawana. I advised her that she was probably correct, but I hadn't named her Tawana; I named her Twana.

"Well, unfortunately, you're stuck with the name the attending nurse recorded, and if you choose to change it, be my guest, but you'll have to pay for a name change," she snapped.

I asked why I would be expected to pay for a name change because of someone else's error. She looked at me in disgust, as if I had insulted her and gave no response. So my baby girl became Tawana Latrice Bivins on that day. It didn't much matter. I had my beautiful baby girl, and I was as happy as I could be.

I had been saving my money from the time I began pilfering from the convenience store. Before I gave birth, I went uptown to the Bank of Suffolk on East Washington and Main Street and opened a checking account in my name without parental consent, parental signature, or questions about my age. Thinking about my plans, I figured I'd need money when the baby came, and a bank account would give me easy access. When the bank representative saw my big belly, she sneered at me, expressing how unbelievable and disgraceful she thought my situation was. They couldn't fathom a sixteen-year-old giving birth to a child out of wedlock. So before I could open my account, I was subjected to the judgment of the white folks who looked down on me because of my circumstances. I didn't learn until years later that their daughters got pregnant out of wedlock, too. Only, they either aborted them, had shotgun weddings, or put the babies up for adoption. They shouldn't have been passing judgment on me as if their lives were perfect. I was on a mission, so I ignored them. I didn't care what they said or thought, as long as I was accommodated. I knew they wouldn't refuse my money.

While I steadily fed the account with money from the convenience store and a few other dollars I received from Sonny, I went back over my plans in my head. I knew I was leaving Suffolk; I just didn't know when.

The money came in handy and I needed it quicker than I had anticipated. Early one evening, when Lewis was in another one of his foul moods, I made a snap decision that I was ready and needed to leave that cursed house. My mother had been ill again. She'd recently had that hysterectomy she so desperately needed. During that time, having that kind of surgery meant cracking open the entire chest cavity from just between the breasts to down by the belly button. She had staples in her and had not completely healed because she'd only been home for a day or so. Lewis arrived home looking for his dinner, as usual. When he didn't find it, he snatched her from the bed, threw her onto the floor, and stomped her in the stomach to teach her a lesson about not having his food prepared when he arrived home. Naturally, I helped her up, and under my breath, I prayed that God would send Lewis to hell. He didn't contest my helping her. In fact, without saying it, he appeared to want me to help her. The now open wound had begun bleeding because several of the staples were loosened from the stomping. The bleeding didn't seem to be too bad, so I helped her up and tried to get her back in bed. She contested because she knew if she didn't cook for him, there would be more trouble.

I offered to do it, but she reminded me, "No. You know he ain't gonna eat your cooking." So half bent over, dressed in pain, she struggled her way to the kitchen to try to prepare his dinner.

He went out and returned about an hour later. When he entered the house, he immediately went to the kitchen and saw that the food wasn't quite ready. He asked, "Bitch, where my motherfucking food? It better be ready, or I'mma beat yo' ass."

She was in the process of going to the back porch to put garbage into the swill can when he came up behind her and kicked her out the back door. She fell hard on her back and struggled to get up. And once she managed to, he and I both were out the door with her. I was trying to get to her to help her, while he was trying to get to her to beat her even more. He got to her first. She was standing, facing the inside of the house. He punched her in the back, and she went crashing down face first, landing on the narrow part of the step, horizontally crossing her windpipe. It temporarily cut off her air supply and she began gasping for air. He pistol whipped her, splitting her head just behind the right ear, where there was another old scar from a previous beating. The blood ran freely from the old wound. I was panic stricken because I thought my mom would die.

He stepped over her and went back inside. I helped her up and got her as far as the sofa in the front room. She needed a doctor, and I tried to get one.

I picked up the telephone to call the ambulance when Lewis yelled, "Put down my damn phone."

"But she's really hurt, and she needs to go to the hospital. Please, Daddy, let me call an ambulance."

"Hell nah! Let the bitch die."

I ran from the house to the only place I knew to go, Mr. Viny's across the street. Mr. Viny was a no-nonsense, serious man who minded his business but demanded the respect of everyone in the neighborhood. He and Lewis were about the same build, weight, and height. The difference was that Mr. Viny didn't make it a point to bully people or threaten them. But if he did threaten someone, he made good on it. Mr. Viny dragged his ulcerated legs when he walked. His legs were always bandaged, and when his pant legs were up, the blood-soaked bandages showed. When he changed the bandages on his front porch, sometimes we children looked because we had never seen anything like it before. He was a nice man and always treated me like a child was supposed to be treated. I was in his house a lot because I was friends with his stepdaughter, so it wasn't a stretch for me to call on him out of desperation when my mom was in trouble.

I begged him, "Please, Mr. Viny, come quick. My mama is hurt real bad, and Daddy won't let me call the ambulance for her. She just got out of the hospital, and she too sick to cook, but he wants her to cook anyway. She can't, so he started beating on her again. Please help us. I think he might kill her."

Mr. Viny was around Lewis's age. He was a dark-skinned man with a large, round face and baldhead that shined like a malt ball. He was a wise, soft-spoken man of few words and feared no one, not even Lewis. In fact, he was the only person I knew who put fear in Lewis's heart. Lewis revered him in every way. I never heard him say a harsh word about or to Mr. Viny. And they both carried guns. Lewis flaunted his while Mr. Viny did not. He walked softly and carried a big stick.

Mr. Viny followed me to our house. Obviously ailing, he ambled in just in time to stop Lewis from further harming my mom. "Lewis, stop beating on that woman. Can't you see she already sick? What's wrong with you?"

But Lewis chose to ignore him and proceeded to go after my mom, anyway. As he attempted to grab her from the sofa, Mr. Viny said, "Lewis, I'm warning you. You know I don't play, and if I have to tell you again not to hit that woman, I'll blow your brains out and be done with it."

Lewis stopped in his tracks. To save face, he said, "Viny, you know you wrong. You know you ain't got no business telling me how to run my house."

"And you got no business beating a sick woman. What she do so bad that you got to beat her while she sick?"

"That ain't yo' business."

"Well, I'm making it my business now because she can't help herself, and you done lost your mind."

He beckoned for me to come to him. "Gal, pick up that phone and call the ambulance."

"Yes sir, Mr. Viny. Thanks."

Before long, the ambulance was there, and my mom and I were on our way to Obici Memorial Hospital. When we arrived, she needed stitches behind her ear as well as replacement staples to reclose her surgical wound. Her windpipe was swollen but not seriously or permanently damaged. My mind temporarily left the hospital, and I began to wonder about what was going to happen when we went back home. I knew there would be a price for both of us to pay—me for having called Mr. Viny and my mom for still having not cooked. I cringed at the thoughts, and it made me nauseous, so my mind trailed back to the hospital.

As I regained control of my thoughts, I looked up and saw two police officers approaching. The emergency room doctor had summoned them. They began asking probing questions, which I welcomed because I thought, now, we could finally get something done about the domestic violence that weighed on me almost as much as her. But then I became confused. I didn't understand why my answers were different from hers.

I said, "Yes, my stepfather did this."

But my mom said, "No, Officer, I walked into a door."

I spit out my words like hot food. "Mom, what are you saying? Tell them the truth; they can help us."

"I *am* telling the truth. Officer, don't pay her no mind. She likes to make up stuff."

I couldn't believe what I was hearing. "Did I make up that scar behind your right ear? Did I make up the missing staples, too?" This time, the words tumbled off my tongue. Turning to the two officers, I said, "Can't you do something about this? My stepfather did all this. And when we get home, he's going to do it some more just because we came for help. Can you help us, please?" I pleaded.

One of the officers said, "I'm sorry, but there's nothing we can do. Your mother has to press charges. You can't because you're a minor."

I plopped down in the seat next to the hospital bed and put my face in my hands, sobbing uncontrollably. I knew I'd have another difficult night. Suddenly, my mind began to race back to my plan. I decided to keep my original notion of leaving. I'd give this thing one last shot. If something happened that evening, I would surely leave without question, with or without my mom and sister.

I wondered how we'd get home from the hospital. But when we got outside, Lewis was waiting, acting as if he had no idea what happened and he was eager to help. We rode in the car in silence. The remaining part of the evening went by without incident.

CHAPTER 28

Final Jeopardy

I was allowed to go two doors down the next evening to a friend's house. Her name was Rosemary. She was an adult who had two small children. We had become good friends, and she invited me over for a spaghetti dinner. Tawana was fast asleep in her bassinet at our house, so my mom said it would be all right to go.

After being there for about forty-five minutes, Annette came to get me. "Phyllis, Ma said come on home because Daddy mad because you left the house."

I apologized to Rosemary for not being able to eat my dinner and left. The closer I got to the house, the faster my heart raced. I never knew what fate awaited me. I entered the house and knew immediately there had been some kind of struggle because my mom's face had ballooned, and her eyes were red from crying. I asked what was wrong. She responded with the usual, "Nothing is wrong. Just go in there and get ready for bed."

"But Ma, I didn't eat any supper yet. You called me home before Rosemary fixed the plates."

Irritated, she said, "Don't worry about it, Phyllis. Just go to bed, please!"

I knew I should've done what I was told because something awful had begun and probably wouldn't finish until the wee hours of the morning. Once in bed, I heard them during the night, arguing, fussing, and fighting. I lay there scared and half-crazy with wonder and fear because my baby was in that room. My mom insisted that the bassinet be kept in her room because she said I slept too soundly and might not hear the baby if she cried during the night. But she also wanted her in there with her because we had chinches, and she didn't want the baby to be subjected to them. Having the baby in my mom and stepfather's room made me uncomfortable because of how unstable Lewis was. I lay listening to them going at it and my baby crying, until suddenly, I heard my mother scream, "Lewis, no!"

There was a gunshot.

My mother screamed, "No, not Angel! Lewis you done killed my grandbaby!"

I couldn't move. My mind stole my reflexes. I lay there paralyzed and in the fight of my life, trying to make my mind and body cooperate with me. I knew I had to get up; I had to move. I needed to be with my baby no matter what. I needed to know that she was all right. But in my heart, I believed she was dead. Finally, the thief released my body, and I slowly rose from my bed in a zombie state, walking to my mother's bedroom. My legs and knees were like water. I had to hold the wall to get to the room.

When I entered, Tawana's tiny brown body lay still in the bassinet. Her eyes were wide open, but she wasn't moving. There was a large hole about the size of a dime in the upper right side of the bassinet. I reached for the little bed and shook it. Finally, totally released from my shock, I screamed while violently shaking the bassinet.

"Tawana, Tawana, cry! Please cry. God, please don't let my baby be dead."

She let out a loud, long cry. A wonderful song of tears. And I was never more relieved. She was alive! My baby was alive and well. Now, I knew what I had to do. This was the final jeopardy. I lost all fear because God had answered my prayer. I very deliberately went to my room, packed my things, gathered all my baby's things, put everything inside the bassinet, and prepared to leave. My mother cried, she pleaded, and did what she could to keep me from leaving, but I told her I could no longer stay there with the threats Lewis posed. My plan only included saving money and leaving. I hadn't determined where I would go yet. But suddenly, that wasn't as big of an issue as I thought.

Once packed, Lewis simply said, "Go on. Get out. And don't think you're gonna come back, because once you gone, you gone."

I never said one word. I left with my baby. We went to Rosemary's for the night. I explained to her what happened, and she understood. I told her I would be leaving in the morning. To go where, I didn't know.

The next morning, after I thought Lewis had gone to work, I sent Rosemary to make sure he was gone. She pretended to come to borrow a cup of sugar. And while there, she saw Lewis, so she struck up a conversation with Mom and learned that he wouldn't be going to work that day. When the news reached me that he hadn't gone to work, I knew something different had transpired during the night. He'd probably questioned Mom about where I was going and if she had any plans to join me. Staying home meant he could be close to the situation and watch. But knowing he was home meant I needed a plan B.

I sat in Rosemary's living room at the window for hours, waiting for him to leave. Finally, a break. I saw his car coming down the street past Rosemary's house, driving up to the corner and turning right onto Cemetery Street. I inched out the door, peeping cautiously to make sure he was out of sight. When I didn't see the pale green and white Chrysler anymore, I quickly scurried out the door and dashed down to my former home. I took one leap from the bottom of five steps, and I was on the screened porch. I entered the house, where I found my mom sitting on the side of her bed, contemplating.

In a huff, I said, "Ma, you have to get out of here."

She stood up fast, as if startled by my presence, and began crying. "Where were you? I didn't know if something happened to you or what. Where is Angel? Is she all right? Where did you sleep last night with that baby? She don't need to be out in the night air. She's only five weeks old." The questions came fast like pinballs jetting out into every direction.

I only answered one question. "We spent the night at Rosemary's. Come on, Ma. You got to get out of here before he comes back. He's going to end up killing you like he did Miss Ruth and those other people. I got some money saved up. The four of us can go to Aunt Ida's in New Jersey. But we must hurry." I hadn't spoken to Aunt Ida in years, but because she was Mom's baby sister, I figured she wouldn't turn us down considering the circumstances.

"You know Lewis ain't gonna let me leave. He riding around with that pistol on his hip and that rifle in the back of the car. He said if I tried to leave him, he'd kill me and Annette. He went to see about getting some more corn liquor for the house early this morning just before daybreak, and he made me go with him. He left again, and he'll be back in a few minutes, and he'll be arguing again. I don't know if I can keep him out of the house long enough to get some things together so I can leave. But I'll try." She sounded so sad.

I had an idea. "I know! Why don't you get him into an argument and make him mad enough to leave the house without you?

Then while he's gone, we can get a taxi to the bus station and go to Aunt Ida's. But you need to start packing and give your stuff to me to save time."

"I don't know if that'll work, but I'll try. I don't want to make him too mad with that gun on him." "Okay. I'm going back to Rosemary's. When I see him come and go again, that'll be our time. Maybe by then, we can even get a ride lined up from somebody. I'll see if Rosemary knows anybody. Do you think you can do this, Ma? If you can't, let me know because I have to do this with or without you."

She walked over to me, held my face in the palms of her hands, and said sweetly, "I won't let you down. I know you want to do better than me. I don't blame you for that. I won't let you down, okay?"

"All right, Ma. I'm depending on you to keep your word."

"How much money do you have? Is it enough to get us all the way to New Jersey? Have you called Ida? S'pose she say no. Then what?"

Assuredly, as if I were the mother, I said, "Ma, don't worry about that. The first thing we need to do is get out of here before he comes back after leaving mad. Can you do that? Then I'll tell you the plans. I've thought about this all night."

Lewis came back before we realized it. When we heard the car door slam, we both panicked.

Mom said, "Run out the back door and cut 'cross Miss Turner's yard and go to Rosemary's back door. Hurry up; he's coming."

I moved like a speeding bullet, and once at the back porch, I didn't bother to take the steps. I leaped from the porch to the ground in a single bound, and in no more than ten seconds, I was banging frantically at Rosemary's back door. She came quickly and opened the door. I fell in hurriedly and began blurting out the decision to move my family out of that madness. Rosemary was able to reach a friend of hers who had a car. He agreed to come pick us up on demand.

After about an hour, I didn't need to know when Lewis left, the sound of the screeching tires and dust he left behind when he sped out of the driveway confirmed his departure. The plan had worked. Now I had to put the next part of it into action.

Excited, I ordered, "Rosemary, call your friend. I'm going to help my mom get her things out of the house."

I ran back to the house and burst through the door, only to find my mom badly beaten and crying. But she was packing her things into the one suitcase we had for the entire family. Anything that needed to go but didn't fit went into brown paper bags. My nerves were skipping rope. We didn't have time to address her pain or how she was able to get him to leave. We moved quickly like an assembly line, getting all we could take in the suitcase and bags. When we were done, we both took one last look at the rooms in the house. I stood in the middle of the front room, turning around, looking slowly, almost nostalgically. My mom looked too as she whimpered from freshly inflicted wounds.

Reality set in, and we knew it was time to move because we didn't know what time he would return. Mom ordered Annette to grab her coat and hat and head out the back door with us. Exiting through the back door was added security in the event our paths crossed with Lewis's before we could reach Rosemary's. We escaped hell and arrived safely two doors down to freedom. It felt like we had traveled miles away. We still had to be cautious, though, because he could return at any moment, and we both knew it didn't matter who was helping us because Lewis would be like an attack dog to them just as he had been to us. We didn't need to scare off our only means of transportation, so we were extra careful.

Phyllis's biological father, Ernest, and his wife, Dorothy (1966-1970)

CHAPTER 29

A New Normal

We had Rosemary's friend drive up to her driveway, which was between Miss Turner's house and hers. He pulled as close to the back of the house as he could. We brought our things out and put them into his trunk and the backseat. Once everything was in the car, I said goodbye to Rosemary and gave her a huge hug and a big thank you with a tearful wave. My mom thanked her, too.

Rosemary said, "Miss Geneva, don't mention it. I'm glad you're getting away from Mr. Lewis because he's a maniac. Y'all will be all right. Y'all take care, and I ain't seen y'all." She smiled and hurried us along.

Somehow, her words sounded parental and wise. They reminded me of a conversation we'd had once when she shared with me that she wasn't afraid of Lewis, and she would kill him if he ever put his hands on her. There was something sinister about the way she'd said it. And I believed her. After all, Rosemary was well known in our little community, well liked, well respected, and known for not taking crap from anybody, regardless of their age or gender.

The car cautiously inched out of the driveway onto the street, and we spotted the green and white Chrysler turning on Roy Street as we headed out. As if on cue, Mom abruptly ducked into the back seat, where she had positioned herself with Annette. I was sitting in the front since this was my plan. I held Tawana confidently in my arms. As we passed him, I looked him straight in the eye like I had never done before, with a serious countenance. I even broke the rule of respect by turning my head as we slowly moved past each other, keeping my eyes fixed on him for as long as I could see him. The dirt road we used to think was too long was now a short path, for I relished the look and felt, for the first time in the five years I had known him, that I had the power. In a strange way, I felt a small sense of vindication. I was now the intimidator. And I was finally in control of my own life.

I wondered when Mom would ask again about our plans. As we approached the Trailways/Greyhound Bus Terminal down on Saratoga Street, it finally dawned on her that she had no idea where we were going. We had talked about going to Ida's, but nothing was confirmed. However, I had taken care of that, too. We reached the bus depot and thanked Rosemary's friend and kept thanking him as we removed our things from the car. We attempted to pay him, but he wouldn't hear of it.

Once inside, I said, "Ma, I have to go to the bank."

"For what?" she questioned.

"I need to get the money I told you I have saved up. I'll be right back."

She didn't worry about that so much because the bank was a ten-minute walk from the bus station. I closed out my account, taking all $250, looking at it in amazement. I had never had that much money in my hands at one time. It felt good, and it gave me a sense of security. With the cash folded and tucked neatly into the left cup of my bra, as I had been taught to do with money, I walked with purpose and attitude back to the station, where Ma, Annette, and Tawana waited. Mom looked a bit worried because she still had no confirmation of where we were going. For the first time, I was in charge, so she had to depend on me to take care of her. I loved the idea because I wanted to be able to take care of her. She deserved to have someone fuss over her for a change. I sat next to her and laid out my plan.

"This is what we're gonna do. I called Aunt Mary collect. I explained everything to her, and she understood. She called Ida and told her what was going on, and Ida understood, too. We're going to buy three tickets, one for Chesapeake and two for New Jersey. Aunt Mary will meet me and Tawana at the bus station in Chesapeake. She said she would take care of us until you get to Ida's with Annette, get settled in, and send for us. I'll keep a few dollars of this money for food and stuff for Tawana and me. You take the rest with you for food and stuff for you and Annette."

My aunt Mary was the family's matriarch and the oldest of Mom's siblings. She lived in Chesapeake, Virginia with her husband and three children. I had lived with her once before when I was about five when she lived in Norfolk.

When Mom realized how elaborate my plan was, she had no recourse. She was now the daughter of her child and quickly settled into the idea, demonstrating her approval and cooperation by giving a simple, "Okay. This sounds like it'll work. I won't let you down, I promise."

Aunt Mary's house was a far cry from what I'd been accustomed to. She had indoor plumbing and shiny wooden floors, four bedrooms, a living room, kitchen, den, patio, huge back and front yards, and a two-car garage. This was suburbia, not at all like what

I had been experiencing for the last almost seventeen years. I knew we wouldn't be in Chesapeake long, so I planned to make the best of my temporary abodes. I had a proper place to bathe. We had our own bedroom, with no evidence of bedbugs, and I ate meals that required no suspicion. I breathed easily and had plenty of time to sit with my thoughts and consider that faith had made this part of my plan possible, but not easy. So there was no time to rest on my laurels. I had to be ready for the next installment of my plan. I couldn't afford to get comfortable. I was concerned because I didn't know what lay ahead, but I knew I couldn't worry about it because there was no use in worrying about something that may not ever happen.

We received word that Mom and Annette arrived safely at Ida's house in New Jersey. Now, Tawana and I had to get there. Aunt Mary's home was lovely, and it was so good to be in a stress-free environment for a change, but I needed to be out of Virginia completely. I wanted no further dealings with the bitterness I'd found there. So the day after Thanksgiving 1970, I folded Suffolk up and put it behind me. I boarded a Greyhound bus from Chesapeake and left Virginia for good.

I arrived in New Jersey in the early evening. A couple of my cousins came to Journal Square in Jersey City to pick us up from the bus depot. I could finally exhale. I stepped off the bus with my baby in my arms, dressed in a tan full-length faux fur coat from B.D. Laderburg. The coat was warm but had a large, noticeable cigarette burn on the right front near the top. I didn't care; I thought I was wearing real fur. My head was covered by a rayon square scarf, folded in a triangle and tied under my chin. Although it was cold, the best I could do for footwear was a pair of white tennis shoes and stockings that had been twisted and tied at the top just over the knee to keep them up. I thought I looked decent, only to learn later that my appearance made me the butt of several unpleasant jokes from my cousins who were carrying on behind my back. They laughed at me because I looked like a country bumpkin, but they didn't understand from whence I came. They always had the benefit of a sound family unit, including both parents and siblings. I was working toward that goal. Until then, I knew I would continue to be judged and spoken ill of because I was the only one of our first cousins who had a child out of wedlock. In fact, they'd even said, "Better her than me." To my knowledge, none of the children of my mother's seven siblings had babies out of wedlock, at least none of the girls. If any of the boys had children before marriage, it would've been more difficult to know, since men didn't have to reveal that information.

Tawana and I were sent to Rutgers Street in Jersey City with my uncle WT and his girlfriend, Ricky. I knew I was safe there and the stay was temporary. Being with my uncle was reminiscent of our time together when I was a child, visiting him on those weekends when he picked me up from Roy Street in his '57 Chevy. Tawana and I remained with him on Rutgers Street for a short time.

Mom had already begun settling in since she and Annette had been there a few weeks before us. She had secured an apartment and I was encouraged. We moved into the three-room apartment at 100 Van Nostrand Avenue, around the corner from WT and downstairs from my Uncle Roshell, Aunt Margie, and cousins, Hortense and Keith. Finally, some stability, family, and solace. My new home—Jersey City, New Jersey!

CHAPTER 30

A Season of Light and Dark

Things began to progress. I started asking random people about school because I knew I needed to finish. I planned to eventually contact Mrs. Davis and let her know I was in the process of making good on her words to me—I was going to live my gift out loud through education. Eventually, someone told me about Dickinson Accredited Evening High School. I got the address and found my way to 2 Palisade Avenue in Downtown Jersey City via bus. I took a deep breath and walked up to the massive structure and through the doors, proceeding nervously but excitedly to the main office, where I announced I was there to enroll in their program for students who wanted to attend evening classes to complete high school. I finished the paperwork, returned it to Ms. Gregory at the desk, and was told I would hear from them when they received my transcript from my former high school. I left there already feeling like I had accomplished a huge feat, but I still lacked a job.

During the day, I was on Bidwell Ave. in Jersey City, at Ida's, who allowed me to bring Tawana with me to her house while I babysat my infant cousin, Deanna, who was four months older than my baby, and Mona, who was not yet full-day-school age. I was paid fifteen dollars a week, most of which went toward carfare back and forth to Dickinson and food for our family—Mom, Annette, Tawana, and me. Mom was excited about my plans to return to school and happy to babysit Tawana while I attended school five nights a week. At the very least, my hope was that finishing high school would position me to contribute more to improving our lives.

Our apartment on Van Nostrand was a tiny three-room unit. Though the rooms were large enough for one person, there were four of us cramped into that small space. There was a kitchen, bathroom, and one bedroom, and we had to convert the living room into a second bedroom. Mom had a full-sized bed, and I had a twin. Annette slept with her and Tawana slept with me. We made it work. Mom learned about public assistance and was eligible, so she applied to receive a small monthly stipend. It was enough to pay the rent, buy a little food, and provide Annette, Mom, and me with a Medicaid card for medical coverage (Tawana was ineligible at the time), but we didn't qualify for food stamps. That meant having to be frugal with spending so there was adequate food. I did the shopping and found myself buying food items like chicken backs, gizzards, and livers because they were cheap. We ate lots of starch because it, too, was relatively inexpensive. We never bought fruit or fruit juice because it was too expensive. However, we welcomed pre-sweetened Kool-Aid and ate every slice of bread in the loaf, including the end pieces. We bought as many "no-frills" items as we could because it allowed us to get more bang for our buck.

I was now finding my way back into the saddle. I was back in school, studying hard to finish what I had started. Graduation day would be January 24, 1973, and I planned to be front and center. It was more important than ever, since I relocated and had an opportunity to start a new life. This was my official first stop. I lived in that apartment for one year before moving on. Nothing could stop me. I was going all the way up.

Then one rainy Saturday morning, no more than six months after our arrival, while my cousin, Hortense—or Tent as she was affectionately called—was visiting from upstairs as I pressed my mom's hair, our doorbell rang. We never had company, so my mother and I looked at each other and said rhetorically, "I wonder who that could be."

Tent said, "I'll get it. It's probably somebody ringing the wrong bell."

We lived in a four-family dwelling, so it could have been someone for any of the apartments. However, she returned to our apartment with someone in tow. We could hear smidgens of the conversation. The hall was long, and their voices echoed but became clearer as they approached our door. My heart was suddenly drenched in fear. The voice was immediately recognizable. To my utter shock and amazement, in walked the devil himself—Lewis.

Fear laughed at me. I was devastated just by the sight of him. I believed in my heart I had seen the last of him when we left Virginia. But that was no longer my reality.

The first words from my mother's mouth were, "How the hell did you find us?"

"Don't gimme that," he retorted. "You called me and gave me the address."

"That's a lie; I ain't gave you nothing!"

I was surprised and pleased by her response, even though I knew she was the liar. I was surprised because I had never heard her talk back to him before. I was pleased because I didn't want him to think he could come all that way and still boss us around. Maybe this time, she had found herself. Maybe she was strong enough now to keep him in his place.

A familiar anger began to raise its nasty head, and I could smell it as it eased up my nose and into my ears, sending unleashed panic and terror throughout my body. My hands began to sweat. My palms were wet, and my legs were like rubber. I was too nervous to speak. I needed to use the bathroom. Tent didn't know what was wrong. But it was clear to both of us that Mom had given Lewis the necessary information to find us.

I stepped away momentarily to regroup. While in our bathroom, I got myself together and realized this was a new time and place. There were certain things to which I no longer had to be subjected. My mind was racing because I knew I would be expected to say something, even if it was only "Hello." I thought quickly. My first words would not only be expected but would set precedence. Therefore, I had to be clear.

When I returned from the bathroom, I offered a powdery, "Hi, Lewis." I was careful to make sure my words were dry and telling. I was loud enough so everyone had undoubtedly heard it. It was bold and intentional. No "mister," no "Daddy," and no respect, just plain old Lewis because that's all he was. And it felt good. I had liberated myself again in the mist of temporary fear. And I could feel my own power humming through my bones.

He had returned in his green and white '62 Chrysler, from which he began unpacking, inserting his unsolicited stuff into our new lives. I looked on in a quiet resolve that said I was there finding my place and refused to include him. Mom pretended she had nothing to do with any of it, so she never helped him. She didn't understand that her indolence spoke volumes.

His return cramped our style right away. He moved into my mother's bed, forcing Tawana and me to share our twin bed with

Annette. It also meant a decline in our quality of life and the relationship I was trying to rebuild with my mom. Then one night after returning home from school, I learned from Tent that Mom had been drinking heavily again, which was disappointing. And Tent saw her spanking Tawana with a paddle from an old bat 'n' paddleball while she was drunk. Tawana was a year old and getting around quite well. I spoke to my mom about the incident, and she became defensive. I ignored it. But I never forgot it. I knew things were about to get out of hand, and I needed to work on a plan because her reacquaintance with alcohol was a sure sign that she was about to return to a time I had hoped was buried in the past forever. I had to think about planning for my immediate future without the benefit of my mother and sister.

Whenever I had an extra fifty cents or a dollar, I purchased a bath cloth, dishcloth, or whatever else I could get to begin building my hope chest. I also learned of a federally funded self-help program called Neighborhood Youth Corps. To be eligible, an applicant had to be dirt poor and sixteen or older. I was seventeen and poor enough that our mice shared what they had with us.

I found my way up to Neighborhood Youth Corps at One Foye Place, not far from the Journal Square area of Jersey City and close to Dickinson. I completed an application for employment. If accepted, the program would offer me on-the-job training while paying me a small stipend. I interviewed well and was accepted. My first job was at Lafayette Teen Post in Jersey City. The job paid a whopping thirty-five dollars per week, which was music to my ears. It was more than double what Ida had been paying. The opportunity allowed me to give up the babysitting job and get some experience to boot. I couldn't wait to share the news with my mom. She was happy for me, too. Once I began working, I was trained for clerical and light bookkeeping duties. However, it would be short lived. Somehow, my past came back to haunt me.

I never understood it, but being attractive was, in so many ways, a curse. Being attractive and having a nice figure was a double whammy. The very first day I began work, my immediate supervisor, Mr. Robinson, literally chased me around the office. I hated him for it. Why couldn't men chase after women who wanted to be chased? Why couldn't they behave themselves like they expected us to do? It went on for a week, and I finally told my counselor, Karleen Parker, what was happening. She immediately removed me and placed me in Downtown Jersey City at the Department of Working Papers. Now I was getting real experience.

Michelle Petillo was a serious, young white woman who made sure I did what was expected of me. She trained me well in the art of letter writing, how to address people when operating as a public servant, how to use a typewriter, and good phone etiquette. Once my allotted time was up with her, I moved on. Michelle was impressed with my work ethic and gave me a good recommendation for my next training assignment, which was the Hudson County Municipal Courthouse, near Five Corners. I learned many invaluable tidbits there as well. Each of the sites did more than provide work experience; they were also the catalyst for my near future. I made good friends and lots of connections. However, my last site was, by far, the most informative and most important.

I was moved to the Jersey City Medical Center, where I was employed as a receptionist for the Jersey City Medical Center Drug Abuse Program. My immediate supervisor was a wonderful priest by the name of Joe Ochs. He was caring and patient. His secretary was an African American woman who knew her craft well. Mr. Ochs instructed her to teach me everything I needed to prepare me to run that office on my own if I had to. But the real significance was that I was in the hospital with reputable doctors. And it became a true blessing when, one night, I arrived home from school early and found my baby running up and down the hall in our building in only a t-shirt and pamper, with a runny nose and no shoes. It was wintertime and cold enough in the hall for a jacket. I picked her up and took her back into the apartment. Then I noticed that she not only had a bad cold but a rattle in her chest and a temperature. I hadn't noticed it before because, usually, by the time I arrived home from school at around 10:30 or 11:00 p.m., she was sound asleep. I didn't know much about what a baby looked like when she was ill, but something didn't quite look right about her. The next day, I returned to work and went to see one of the pediatricians I had met in the hospital. I described what I observed in my baby and asked him what he suggested. He said, "Bring her in; I'll be glad to look at her for you."

I said in a pleading voice, "She's running a temperature, and I'd have to bring her on the bus after hours because I can't afford to miss work; otherwise, I won't have enough money to get back and forth to work and school before my next paycheck."

"Okay. Where do you live?" he asked.

"At one hundred Van Nostrand Ave."

"I'll be there this evening, and I'll take a look at your baby."

"Okay, thank you so much. What time should I expect you?"

"Around seven."

I couldn't believe my good fortune. I finished my workday, went off to school, and left classes early enough to get home before the doctor arrived. When he came in, he found Tawana still trying to carry on her normal play, but it was obvious she was run down and weak. He picked her up and laid her on our bed, examining her thoroughly.

Finally, he said, "This baby has pneumonia. Take her up to the medical center immediately and tell them I said to admit her."

I followed instructions. We got onto the Greenville Avenue bus and headed up Jackson Avenue (AKA Dr. Martin Luther King, Jr. Dr.) to the Jersey City Medical Center. Once there, I wondered if my word would be adequate or if they wouldn't believe a doctor would have made a house call and given instructions to have my baby admitted. To my surprise, he had done his homework, and all was taken care of before our arrival.

I watched with teary eyes as a nurse slid a little white wristband on her tiny arm. They took her up to the children's ward and placed her in a crib, where she lay still for a while. I sat next to her and played with her cute little hands, remembering when I kissed them for the first time in Obici Memorial Hospital just over a year before. She held onto my index finger tightly. I just sat and cried, wondering if my baby would be all right. The nurse came by and said I had to go. I asked if I could stay a bit longer because Tawana wasn't accustomed to being alone, and she would probably cry if I left. I was granted permission to stay. I fell asleep, and she was still holding my finger when I awakened.

It was late. I had to go home so I could be back there the next day. Part of the blessing was being an employee in the hospital, so I was able to go up to the children's ward as often as I liked. I spent a good portion of my workday there, including my lunch hour, and as much time as I was allowed when I returned in the evening after classes. The security guard always let me up on the elevator. Tawana was there for almost two weeks, and the established routine continued until she was released.

CHAPTER 31

Like Manna from Heaven

I knew it wasn't healthy for my mom to continue keeping Tawana. Since Lewis had come back into her life, she was drinking too much and lacked focus. His presence, his influence, and the alcohol he steadily provided her clouded her judgment. One night, when things weren't going so well because Lewis was trying to be the head of our household, telling not only my mom what to do, but me as well, I spoke up for myself. One thing led to another, and he had the gall to tell me to get out.

I looked him straight in the eyes and said with conviction, "This is not your apartment, and you can't make me go anyplace. This is my uncle's house, and I help pay the rent in this apartment, so I have as much say as my mother, not you." I never flinched. It didn't even dawn on me that he could've struck me at any moment and there may have been little I could do. But I had shed all fear of him.

He threatened to beat me.

As I neared the door, I said, "You want to beat somebody? Okay, I'll be back in a minute with someone you can beat."

I ran upstairs and told my uncle Roshell what happened. He

promptly followed me downstairs into our apartment and said with purposeful authority, "Listen, I don't have nothing to do with whatever domestic problems y'all have, but this is my sister, and my niece, and my house. You're not gonna hit either one of them while I'm alive. If you don't like what I'm saying, you can leave."

Lewis began telling my uncle how I had back talked him. But Uncle Roshell's response was joy to my ears. "Well, you know what? I only put up with you because of my sister, but I never rented this apartment to you, anyway. So you have twenty-four hours to get your stuff and get out of my house. Then you won't have to worry about her talking back. Geneva, you're my sister and you're welcome to stay. I'm not asking you to leave."

"Well, Roshell, if my husband not welcome to stay, then I ain't welcome either. So don't worry, I'll leave your house in twenty-four hours."

"That's up to you. I'm not putting you out, but he's not welcome here."

It was wonderful to hear someone put Lewis in his place and defend me for a change, but I was now in a quandary because my mom gave me an ultimatum. She went back to my uncle and asked if they could stay for another week because they needed time to pack everything up, and he granted her wish.

She said to me, "You still a minor because you only seventeen, so if you don't have a place to live by the time we get ready to leave, you coming back to Virginia with us."

Mom knew I wouldn't be able to afford the rent for that apartment once she left, so I would have to make arrangements for a place to live. I wouldn't dare ask my uncle about retaining the apartment, unless I had no other choice. It would be a huge handout since I would need to secure enough income to maintain the apartment as well as the utilities and living expenses.

The thought of going back to the hell I had escaped sent shockwaves through me. I had to do something. Then my thoughts flew back to my child with warp speed. She was still in the hospital. Where would I go? What would I do? Who would care for my baby? How would I manage? What about school? The questions ran rampantly through my head. I had to think fast and soberly.

The next day when I returned to work, I checked in and went to the children's ward. To my surprise, my baby was being discharged, and that made me happy. I went back upstairs and spoke to Mr. Ochs and asked about the possibility of taking a few hours off to get my baby properly discharged and take her home. I offered to work overtime during the evening to make up the time.

He said, "No, that won't be necessary. Go take care of your baby. If I can do anything to help, let me know."

I went through the standard patient discharge procedure, and everything seemed fine, until the question of money came up.

The clerk asked, "So how will you be paying?"

I looked at her like she had two heads. I didn't have any money. I had assumed because the nice doctor told me to tell them to admit my child, it was somehow gratis. I was tongue tied when I spoke. "I don't have any money."

"What about insurance?" she said kindly.

"I'm sorry, I don't have that either. My mother gets welfare. Does that count?" I gave her my mom's name and other vital information, so she made a phone call.

When she got off the phone, she said, "I called down to the welfare office to verify your mother's information. The clerk established that you, your mother, and your sister are on assistance, but not your child."

No surprise there; however, I wasn't sure what she expected from me since I had no money or insurance. I sat quietly to hear what she would suggest next. The woman looked at my daughter's file then back at me. "Come on. I want to introduce you to someone."

We went across the hall to accounts payable, where an attractive, well-dressed, middle-aged African American woman sat behind her desk, with glasses sitting across the bridge of her nose. Her walnut complexioned face was impeccably made up. She quickly smiled and extended her hand to offer me a chair.

I sat, and the clerk said, "Phyllis, this is Tina. I think she might be able to help you out."

I thanked the woman after she briefly explained my dilemma to Tina.

Tina said, "Sweetheart, the hospital will not release your baby until they know how the bill will be handled."

"But if I don't have money, and you keep her until I get it, it will only increase the bill. Plus, I don't have a way to get this amount of money." The bill was for thousands of dollars, and I was still earning thirty-five dollars a week.

Tina asked, "What about your parents? Can they help?"

"It's only my mom. She gets public assistance. I work, but I only get thirty-five dollars a week, and most of that goes to bus fare to and from work and school because I'm trying to complete my high school education during evenings while working days."

Tina took my information and diverted her attention to some documents that she sifted through. Finally, she pulled a small card from a Rolodex and laid it on her desk. She turned to her typewriter and began typing away. "You know what?" she said. "You and your baby need welfare separate and apart from your mother. Take this letter, and go to this address: One hundred Newkirk St. Give it to the receptionist, and they will assign you a caseworker. The caseworker will give you a case number. Bring that number back to me, and we will release your baby. Do you understand what I'm telling you?"

"Yes!" I said excitedly. And I was off.

The welfare office was in walking distance. I arrived and immediately took care of business. A man who identified himself as a caseworker saw me. I provided the necessary information and was told to wait in an area with several other people who were probably there for similar reasons. I knew immediately that I did not want to remain on welfare. Many of the people in the waiting area looked as if life had beaten them down. Most were women and their faces each told a sad story. If only they knew that they were not victims because they were still here, and there was always an opportunity for them to challenge themselves and look for a better tomorrow.

After about an hour, the caseworker returned, and I followed him back to his cubicle. Once seated, he reviewed the information with me and explained that I should present Tina with the green card he gave me, which was my new Medicaid card. He said he needed me to sign some documents, and I did. He explained that the documents would entitle me to food stamps and a stipend to offset my thirty-five-dollar-a week salary.

I couldn't believe I was receiving such a blessing. I thanked him, and when I got outside, I openly thanked God. I returned to the hospital, gave them the requested information, and waited patiently as preparations were made for me to take my baby home. I caught the Number Three bus for Greenville, went home, and enjoyed my baby for the remainder of the day. I remembered to telephone Mr. Ochs to explain what happened. He was happy for me because he thought I was one who deserved public assistance.

He said, "Don't be embarrassed about this. You are using the system the right way."

I skipped school that night to stay home with my baby because things at home weren't quite right, and I wasn't feeling very trusting.

The next day, I had to return to work and, once again, my baby was home with my mom and her husband. Things were beginning to take on a different tone. I was pensive when I arrived at work that morning. My usual jovial mood was hiding, and everybody in the office noticed.

Mr. Ochs called me into his office. "Sit down," he said. "I've been doing some checking around, and I've been hearing some positive things about you. I'd like to help, if I can. I hear you've been trying to find an apartment because your folks are moving back south, and you want to remain here."

I was surprised by how much he knew. "Yes, that's true, but I don't know where to start looking for a place or where I would get the money to maintain it." I felt comfortable explaining why I couldn't continue living in my uncle's house. He asked if there were any other relatives with whom I could stay. I told him they all had their own families and no extra space.

As I spoke, he fished for a piece of paper and a pen. He scribbled some information on the paper and handed it to me. He said, "Go to this address. You know where Bergen Avenue is, don't you?"

"Yes, it's down the street from where I report on Foye Place to meet my counselor."

"Ask for Mr. Grossman. Show him this piece of paper, and tell him I sent you and I'm asking him to help you in any way he can. Go now, and don't worry about the hours here. You'll still get your pay. Go on."

Tears of joy welled up in my eyes. "Thanks so much, Mr. Ochs. Wow! Thanks a lot."

I left the hospital and walked to Mr. Grossman's office. He was a realtor. I saw the sign hanging from the small opening between two large businesses. I looked up at the sign and compared my handwritten information with the sign's information. Both were the same. I went up what seemed like an endless set of stairs, and once inside the small, brightly decorated office, I asked the office manager if I could see Mr. Grossman.

"Wait just a second, please … Okay, miss, you can go in now. Mr. Grossman will see you."

I thought, *Wow! That was quick.* I entered the room, and Mr. Grossman stood and extended his hand for a handshake then gestured to an awaiting seat. I explained what I needed, which was a cheap place to live in a hurry. He asked me a series of questions, one of which was, "How old are you?"

I hesitated for two reasons. First, I didn't know if he would rent to a minor, and secondly, I wasn't a good liar. As confidently as I could, I said, "I'm eighteen." I wondered what I would do if he asked for identification to prove my age. But he didn't. Instead, we finished the interview, and he said he would telephone my supervisor to check my credentials. Immediately upon completing the interview, I raced to the bus stop and back into the office at Foye Place to tell my counselor, Sam Martin, what just happened.

"Mr. Martin, I'm trying to get an apartment, and I was sent to Mr. Grossman. He'll be calling you to verify some information I gave him. This is what I told him ..."

Mr. Martin said, "You're late. He already called."

My heart sank, and I didn't have the nerve to ask what was said during the conversation. I hung my head and began thinking about life in Suffolk again. But Mr. Martin smiled at me and broke the silence. "I gave him all the right answers. In fact, he said for you to return tomorrow to sign your lease and pick up the keys to the apartment he thinks will be good for you. It's Thirty Atlantic Street."

"Thank you so much, Mr. Martin. I owe you big time. I really appreciate what you did." In the words of my mother, I was "grinnin' like a Cheshire cat."

I left the office floating, a fresh sensation of light slathering over me. I didn't have any thoughts as to whether I would or would not like the apartment. I was only concerned with the fact that I would be getting an apartment—my very own apartment.

The next day, I received a call at work to go to Mr. Grossman's office to sign my lease and pick up my apartment keys. I went during my lunch hour and spoke to the office manager. She asked me to wait for a moment and told me, "Mr. Grossman will see you now."

I was nervous because I was told I only had to see her, sign a lease, pick up the keys, and that was it. Mr. Grossman invited me to sit. I thought, surely, it would be bad news.

"I don't believe for one second that you're eighteen," he said, "but there's something a little different about you, and if Father Ochs sent you, then I'm willing to take a chance on you, too. Normally, I don't rent to anyone under eighteen, but I believe you're a young woman trying to improve her living conditions." He wished me luck, provided the lease for my signature, and gave me my keys.

I thanked him and left.

That evening, I told my mom I would not be going back to Virginia with them. "I found an apartment, and I'll be receiving public assistance until I can do better," I said.

Sadness ripped through her face. Suddenly, I felt sad, too. I was sad that my little sister would be going back to that one-way street called Doomed Road. I was sad that my mom would resume her life of beatings and drinking binges and whatever else awaited. However, I would not allow any of that to cloud my judgment. I was an unfinished painting dancing on my own canvas of life. I had a child for whom I was responsible. I had an opportunity to earn my high school diploma and maybe go to college. I would be the first one in my immediate family to go beyond high school. I had a life I could look forward to. My mind was made up. I was staying the course.

On the day before their departure, I moved into my apartment. I wished Mom could have shared this special time with me, but she couldn't. I forged on, thinking about the only furniture I had, which reminded me of Pond Town. I inherited the twin bed my sister, my baby, and I shared in our three-room apartment. Other than that, I had my hope chest, with six bath cloths, two towels, three dish-cloths, a potholder, a pair of shower curtains, and some mix-matched dishes my mom slipped to me while her husband was occupied with packing the car. She also gave me a sheet, a pillowcase, and a gold bedspread for our bed. I found a few empty mayonnaise jars and brought them along to use for drinking glasses.

The next day, Mom, Annette, Tawana, and I all said our good-byes. It was a tearful occasion. Mom made me promise I'd keep in touch and bring her grandbaby to see her. Through the tears and strained words, I agreed.

Then my mom and my sister were gone, just like that. I felt such gripping pain. I wanted my mom to change her mind and say no to Lewis, to say yes to me, but that wasn't to be.

CHAPTER 32

The Next Installment

I had never been on my own. The new experience was somewhat scary. I was seventeen and the head of my own household, solely responsible for whatever happened to Tawana and me. If I didn't do what I was supposed to, we wouldn't eat and wouldn't have a place to stay, slinging us back in time to a horrible repeat of my past. I shook it off. I knew we'd be okay because I would not be easily broken. I was already making tremendous progress. It just felt different and frightening. I was in a new world, beginning adulthood before time.

The apartment at 30 Atlantic Street was huge. There were four rooms and a full bath. That meant Tawana and I each had our own bedroom. There was a living room, a kitchen, and our twin bed. Things were still looking up.

I met a new friend who reminded me of Rosemary. She was about Rosemary's age, thirteen years my senior. Her name was Barbara Maxwell. Barbara was married to Ernest, and together, they had three sons. They lived down the hall from us on Van Nostrand, and I was glad I had met them before I moved into my new place. We remained friends throughout the years. She looked out for me with sound advice, and she babysat Tawana on occasion. Barbara even told me about a friend of hers who was refurnishing her basement and throwing out her old furniture. She was willing to sell all of it to me for ninety dollars. I jumped at the opportunity. I didn't know what it looked like and I didn't care; all I had was a twin-sized bed. The furniture was in terrible shape, but it became my treasure, accommodating three of my four rooms. Barbara's friend even threw in the delivery for free. The sofa was gray, with a high back and thick cushions. A solid floral print was ingrained into the fabric. It was beat up, but a throw would help. I didn't own one, but I did have an extra sheet I could use. The sheet covered the huge hole on the topside of the sofa. I stuffed old clothes in the opening to keep the springs from sticking people when they sat and put the sheet on top to serve as a throw. The coffee table had mix-matched legs. There were no end tables or lamps. The kitchen came equipped with a refrigerator and gas stove, and a kitchen table with three legs was included in the furniture sale. I had been previously acquainted with a three-legged table. We had one in Pond Town. I eliminated the problem by propping the end with the missing leg onto the windowsill. The table was wooden and had been painted with house paint to cover the peeling and chipping. It was splinter-laden, also reminiscent of the one from Pond Town. I remedied that by using one of the two shower curtains to cover it. I hung the other one in the bathroom. The bedroom was as sparse as the rest of the house. I needed a new mattress and slats, but the box spring and frame were okay. I didn't care. I had my own place.

I was beginning to understand how the system worked. The more I did for myself, the better things became. That fact got me thinking even more seriously about my education. If I had only a high school diploma, I would be limiting myself. I had known since my days back in Virginia that I wanted more so I could feed my intellect and build a better life for myself at the same time. I had a daughter now, who would need to know how to build a life of her own without experiencing the hardships I endured.

By 1972, my training with Neighborhood Youth Corps was complete, and the blessings continued to pour down. I learned that a front office clerk position had opened in Neighborhood Youth Corps at One Foye Place. I was recommended for the job, and I got it. It was my first full-time job with a full salary and benefits. I went from making thirty-five dollars a week to ninety dollars a week. Ninety dollars must have had some magical powers because it kept coming up in my life. My new salary was ninety dollars a week, the cost of the furniture was ninety dollars, and my rent was ninety dollars a month. I reported my new income to my caseworker, and he told me I was still eligible for assistance, but an adjustment would be made to align my income with the national average for a family of two. Now, I had a steady salary, a small subsidy check from welfare to help support my baby and me, and Medicaid and food stamps. My quality of life was increasing rapidly.

One day, when returning from lunch at work, a suited gentleman stood staring at me from the office door of another federally funded program down the hall from mine. Our eyes met and we both spoke to each other simultaneously. I felt something unusual, like a surge of energy that happens when you catch a glance of someone you like, but I let it slide. During our next perchance meeting in the hallway, we spoke again and engaged in small talk. He told me his name was James Ray, and he asked if I worked in the building. I told him I did and pointed to the sign over the door. I asked the same, knowing the answer, and he said yes, he, too, worked in the building, and he was the executive director of the federally funded program for which he worked. From that day, we spoke often because his door was always open, so we'd see each other in passing.

One day, he invited me to lunch. I accepted the invitation, and we began dating soon after. During one of our initial conversations, I learned that he was nine years my senior and in a rocky relationship, but that didn't matter because this seemed like a sudden moment of happiness. I wanted to savor the feeling, for whatever it was worth. We had many more lunch, dinner, and drink dates, parties and vacations. He knew I was completing my high school education and encouraged me to do well and continue. He even began driving me to school after work and picking me up. Our courtship evolved into a love affair that lasted thirteen years. He became a full-time father to Tawana, the only father she ever knew. He loved her and she loved him. Our relationship and family unit were as solid as it could be, with the usual ups and downs. We had great times together at home and on vacations.

On January 24, 1973, graduation day had finally come, an important milestone for me. I received the pin for newspaper editor in chief, and I was inducted into the National Honor Society, garnering respect and acknowledgements from my classmates. Each step was an accomplishment met with enthusiasm and a hunger to go after the next phase in my quest for education and the next installment into a solid future.

The graduation class ballot from our yearbook, *The Owl*, honored me with eight out of twenty-four categories: most popular girl, class beauty, most ambitious girl, humorist, stenographer, best school spirit, best dressed girl, and class pals, along with my friend, Karen Davis. The category I most cared about was "most ambitious girl." My peers recognized my thirst for what was beyond high school. Though some may have considered the title frivolous, I took it seriously because the two years I had invested advanced my thinking and made me even more inquisitive and eager to learn. My aspirations were being challenged and my curiosity had been whet. I was ready to move forward in the world of academia. I had excelled throughout my two years at Dickinson and was looking forward to the next chapter my gift had to offer. It was exciting. But, in some ways, it felt ethereal, and I couldn't help thinking it wasn't real and something would happen to interrupt my euphoria.

I did my part. I extended invitations to my family, completed all graduation paperwork and submitted it on time, and I picked up my cap and gown as instructed. When the time came, I took a deep breath before entering the auditorium for my farewell. I looked out from the stage and saw James and my aunts Margie, Edith, and Mildred. Mom was noticeably missing. She should have been there to cheer me on and hold Tawana for me. Instead, Aunt Margie held her because Mom couldn't make it. She told me she had no money and no means to get to Jersey. I couldn't afford to send for her, and I knew Lewis wouldn't permit her to come. He feared my influence would keep her there. He understood that I had the power. I had freed myself from him and no longer feared him. I had also completed high school—more than he ever dreamed of doing. Most of all, I hadn't accomplished this feat for its sake. I had done it so I'd never allow anyone to prop his boot on my neck again.

Daughter Tawana (age one) and Phyllis (1971-1973)

Daughter Tawana during the first Christmas in our first apartment

Phyllis, high school graduation (1973)

CHAPTER 33

The Fast Track

The first step was complete. I was college bound. However, before considering college, while on vacation in Virginia visiting my mom and sister in July of 1973, I became pregnant. James and I were both excited about the news. I continued working throughout March. I now had a social life, with lasting friends who had positive influences on me, and they gave me a surprise baby shower.

On April 20, 1974, at Margaret Hague Hospital in Jersey City, I gave birth to my second healthy baby girl, Zammeah Monique Bivins. Young and healthy, I returned to work by the end of May.

In July of 1974, I left Neighborhood Youth Corps for a promotion at Hudson County Family Planning five months before turning twenty one years old. I was hired as an administrative assistant, the youngest to hold the position. Mr. Carlton Lovett, my boss at Neighborhood Youth Corps, had arranged for the promotion. I settled in immediately, handling the responsibilities of building management, the company car, and the alarm system. I became well known and respected in an office of doctors, nurses, and lab technicians, who were all my seniors.

Compliments on my work ethic from those who worked in the same office were often the topic of conversation with my boss, John Randolph, who, like his friend, Carlton Lovett, was the executive director. I was happy with the work I was doing; however, I wasn't satisfied. But that would soon change because I was still on the fast track.

A guidance counselor from high school back in Virginia had made clear that I should not concern myself with college. I was encouraged to take home economics and other subjects designed for those who aspired to stay home and have babies. Outside of my teachers, I saw few other examples. I thought life only offered what my counselor had suggested. But this new fast track offered so much more. I was determined, more than ever, to continue moving upward. I worked extra hard to prove my worth. I looked for ways to improve myself and align with the medical professionals around me who were not shy about sharing their expertise and opinions regarding my inquiries about work, life, and furthering my education.

I found myself in a continuous state of malcontent where my lack of education was concerned. Having just a high school diploma wasn't enough. It made me feel uneasy and inadequate. And sitting in my office doing my job became repetitive. I could do it with my eyes closed. I needed a challenge, and I believed higher education, as I had come to know it through research and conversations with those who were educated, would be just the challenge I needed. I felt my internal motivation speaking to me. I listened and, once again, began looking for ways to improve my situation even more. I continued to remind myself that I needed to be a role model for my children. I didn't want them to see a woman with my potential stop at a high school diploma when she aspired to be so much more.

One day, as I sat at my desk typing a monthly report for John, I said to him, "John, I've completed your report. I'll be back in a bit. I need to take care of something, so I'll be taking an extended lunch."

I left the building and got into my first car, purchased with an income tax return, a yellow and black 1968 Ninety-Eight Oldsmobile. I drove down to Kennedy Boulevard and parked in front of Saint Peters College. I went in and inquired about enrollment.

The office manager quickly assessed my situation and said, "I'm sorry, but there is no more financial aid available. You might try Jersey City State College further up the boulevard."

I left feeling put off but not defeated. After all, she had suggested a second college. I went inside and asked the same question, but I was met with the same quick reply. It came as a surprise, and it upset me. This time, I had no other options.

I stood, dumbfounded. With a quivering voice, I said, "How is it that there's no financial aid available? I see every day on the television commercials where students are told to go to the college and just apply because the money is there. Well, I'm here, and now you're saying there's no money." The quivering voice turned into an unexpected bout of open weeping.

The woman in the front office said, "Wait a minute, sweetheart. Take a seat. I'll be right back." She went into an office and returned about five minutes later. "Go in to see Mr. McGhee. He's the director of admissions."

I went in still whimpering. He invited me to sit and asked me what the problem was. I reiterated the earlier conversation and added, "I don't understand why we are told all we have to do is apply. Here I am. I'm trying to apply, and now I'm told that no such funds exist. I can't sit behind a typewriter all my life. I have to do something else. And now that I've made that decision, no one wants to help me."

Mr. McGee said, "Do you really want to go to school that badly?"

I held my head up and looked him in his eyes. "Yes, more than anything in the world."

"Wait a minute. Let me see what I can do. Wait in the outer office for a moment."

He flipped through the Rolodex on his desk as I left his office. I heard him making a call and asking questions.

He summoned me back into his office. "Okay, so you want to go to college?" he asked.

I nodded.

"This is the situation. There are some funds available from a program called BEOG (Basic Education Opportunity Grant). The stipulation, however, is in order to take advantage of these funds, you must enroll in college as a full-time student. Didn't you say you work?"

"Yes, but I worked days while I finished high school full-time in the evenings. I know college will be more challenging, but I'm up for it. Is there a way I can go full-time evenings?"

"Yes, but it means you'll be here Monday evening through Thursday evening, and you must take a minimum of twelve credits at all times to maintain your full-time status. Less than twelve credits would disqualify you for the grant."

"I can handle that. How long do I have to repay the grant, and when can I start?"

"Well, to answer your first question, because the BEOG is a grant, it doesn't have to be repaid. But the grant may not cover everything, so you can also apply for a federal loan. You can go to the financial aid office, and someone there will assist you with that part of the process. You can begin spring '75."

"What is that?"

"That's our January session. Once we get you registered, we will make sure you have all the information you need."

"Mr. McGee, how long will it take me to complete the courses for a degree?"

"If you go full-time during the day, it takes four years. But because you will be attending full-time evenings and taking the minimum credits to give you full-time status, it could take you about six years, maybe a little less if you attend during our summer and winter sessions."

"If it takes four years to be done, I'll be close. Mr. McGee, thank you very much. You don't know how much this means to me. And watch, I'm going to make you glad you made this decision. You'll see."

"I think I do know how much it means. If I can do anything else just let me know. Here, take one of my cards." He smiled.

I turned back to him once I reached his office door and said, "I'm going to make you real proud."

Daughter Zammeah and Phyllis (1974)

CHAPTER 34

Relationships!

When I enrolled into Jersey City State Teachers College, Zammeah was nine months old and Tawana was four years and three months. It was a new experience with new adjustments. There was no need to pack up for a dorm because the school was nearby; besides, I had two children, so I needed different living arrangements. I wondered what my freshman year would be like. I felt giddy and panicked, but I quickly relinquished any thoughts of distress, remembering my love for school and recognizing that I could become quite comfortable making student life a career for myself.

I soon left Hudson County Family Planning because, like many other federally funded programs during that time, it had been cut. By April 1975, I sat at a new desk at the Department of Public Works as a clerical aide, a position I knew well. But I wasn't at all comfortable because my previous experience had prepared me to be much more than an aide. I quickly proved myself and was promoted to administrative assistant with the Division of Streets and Sewers. I was now under another federally-funded program called

CETA (Comprehensive Employment Training Act), where my salary, including welfare, jumped to a grand total of $10,000 a year. I had landed, purely by accident, a decent apartment in a decent neighborhood, and my older daughter was in Catholic school, the younger one in nursery school. We still weren't living on Easy Street. I worked from nine to five Monday through Friday and attended evening classes at the college Monday through Thursday from 5:30 to ten p.m.

While James and I were still in a relationship, in many ways, his so-called rocky relationship with the other woman turned out to be one that—in his words—would take some time to end. Their relationship had begun long before I was a thought. They had gotten together because she was pregnant. Along the way, he was hooked on heroine for five years and she supported him through recovery. Now that he had gotten his life back on track and was reintroduced into society, he credited her for supporting him and did not feel it would be right to leave her. Then there was always the thought of his son, a child older than my girls. We often discussed his departure from his other relationship. He insisted he was working on it and finding it difficult to walk away from his son, who was having a variety of issues in and outside of school. Eventually, I gave him an ultimatum. He opted to move in with us, and we remained together for thirteen years.

While James was still with the other woman, I had a bit of a set back and had to take a short hiatus because I became ill and needed surgery. I couldn't depend on James to help me, so there was no one to care for my two small children during my hospital stay. I reached out to Mom for help. She responded by moving the entire family back to Jersey, including Lewis. This time, however, he had grown older and was supported by a walking frame due to a stroke he'd suffered while they were still in Virginia. So his return was absent the violent outbursts and ugly rants he used to dole out. Eventually, Mom could no longer care for Lewis. He left Jersey City and took up his final days somewhere in the Carolinas with his daughter, Adelaide.

After surgery, when I was ready to return to work, I tried to reacquaint Mom with her first grandchild and introduce her to her second one, so we agreed to try babysitting again while I attended classes. It worked for a while. Mom seemed to remain sober long enough for me to get back on my feet and continue my classes. Unfortunately, she fell off the wagon again, leaving me with plenty of nights to pack a bag of books, crayons, coloring books, and snacks so I could bring the girls with me to class. The girls were well-mannered and welcome in the classroom. They sat in the back of the room and occupied themselves with their goodies.

Finally, the day came when I was asked to declare a major. I hadn't considered in what field my degree would be. I met with an academic advisor, who helped me look at the courses I had taken. To my surprise, and without direction, I had taken several education courses, enough, in fact, to declare a major in education.

I decided to go into education and develop the seeds Mrs. Davis had planted back in 1962, when I was a mere third grader. I wanted to become an elementary school teacher and a change agent for children, as she had been for me. I felt confident that I would be that teacher because I had firsthand experience of Mrs. Davis's example. She nurtured me, guided me, and encouraged me to express and develop my gifts. I had programmed myself to do just that.

Once I determined my major, I was scheduled to do my junior practicum and student teaching as a full-time day student, so I quit my job and became totally dependent on welfare. I had work-study, which provided me with pocket change, but getting to school and work daily without a car with two small children was challenging.

My Ninety-Eight Oldsmobile had died a slow and painful death after three years. The repairs were too much for me and had begun draining my bank account, so I had to let it go and return to public transportation until I could do better. I managed. I collected the little bit of car insurance money and used it wisely because I could see the end of the tunnel. Where we lived, I feared I would lose my children to the streets, so I relocated. This meant rising every morning between four and 4:30 a.m. to get to the bus stop two blocks from my house in time to catch the 5:30 a.m. Number 21 bus out of East Orange to Penn Station for an eight a.m. class in Jersey City. I traveled with two babies, one in my arm still asleep and the other in tow, holding onto my leg. Once at Penn Station, we took the World Trade Center Train into Jersey City Journal Square. Then we boarded the Jackson Avenue bus to Kearney Avenue Day Care Center, where I dropped off my baby before boarding the Bergen Avenue bus to Jackson and Bayview Avenues to Sacred Heart School to drop off Tawana.

Once I saw Tawana inside the building, I made a fifteen-minute walk through an alleyway to Kennedy Boulevard and across campus to class. On the days when I hadn't arrived by 7:45 a.m., my instructor, Mrs. Lillian Sachs, knew I'd had transportation issues, so she would set up two desks in the back of the classroom, where I would put the baby until my first break of the morning. The class was an all-day lab from eight a.m. to three p.m. The first break was reserved for taking the Bergen Avenue bus to the day care center to drop Zammeah off, get her settled in and take the next bus back on the opposite side of the street in time to return to class before the short break ended. The transportation issue would only last two years. I was able to use residual money from my grants, loans, and tax refund to purchase another used car for $2,000.

CHAPTER 35

The Good and the Bad with the Ugly

When I was scheduled to do student teaching, I was excited because it meant finally getting into a classroom, putting the theory into practice, and interacting with real students. I was assigned to Martin Luther King Elementary School in Jersey City. The excitement of being in a seventh-grade classroom gave me a warm feeling. I met the children and immediately saw myself in many of the boys and girls. But this class of students was different from my experiences in one major way—the children were terrified of their teacher. She sat at her desk and barked at the children all day. Some of them responded like robots, while others flinched every time she spoke. One little boy even resorted to urinating on himself rather than ask to go to the restroom. For the first week, I sat in the back of the room and observed everything. Then the day came when I was allowed to flex my muscles. I had planned my lesson and was overwhelmed with excitement about executing it. My cooperating teacher complimented me, explaining in detail what a good job I had done for my first time teaching. I loved the feeling I got from the experience. I felt empowered as I imparted knowledge to a group of eager students.

The days went by, and I was allowed more and more autonomy until, finally, I was given complete control over the class. I planned well, asked my cooperating teacher all the right questions, and delivered great lessons. My diligence earned me a seat at the table. That meant moving from the kidney table in the back of the room to a student desk next to my CT (cooperating teacher), indicating to the students that I was her equal. We discussed students, grades, projects, my skillsets, future lessons, and even the possibility of a recommendation for hire at the school once I graduated. She even commented on how professional and well-dressed I was. Most of all, she said the students loved and respected me.

She wrote a full report and put it in my file. My college supervisor shared the report with me and expressed how impressed she was with the kind of work I had been doing. She encouraged me to continue.

One day, while in class, I was interrupted by an unfamiliar smell seemingly emitting from the baseboard. I mentioned it to my CT, explaining that the smell was strong, and I was asthmatic and having trouble breathing in the odor. Together, we tried to figure out what it was, but to no avail. Then during lunch one day in the teacher's lounge, a teacher asked me how things were going with my CT. I talked about how I was enjoying the experience but having trouble breathing at the front of the room because there was an awful smell coming from the baseboard. She and a couple of her colleagues laughed. When lunch was over, I returned to the classroom, but just as I was about to enter, one of the teachers said, "Good luck" and laughed again. I thought nothing of the comment. However, the next day, my CT appeared standoffish. I couldn't figure out why. She wouldn't speak to me, and she refused to give me an assignment. I wasn't allowed to teach, and she sent me back to the kidney table. Without warning, my supervisor came to the classroom and asked to speak to me in the hall. She informed me that I would be leaving the school and relocating to a new one. She explained that my CT had written a second report expressing her disappointment with my performance. She said my lessons were not aligned with the school's, I refused to listen to instruction, didn't receive criticism well, was always late to class, my hair was never properly groomed, my clothes were wrinkled, and I looked unkempt in general. She even reported that she would do whatever it took to prevent me from getting a license to teach, even if it meant taking the letter to Trenton herself.

I was confused. I didn't know where this was coming from. The next day, I reported to my new location, A. Harry Moore School for the Deaf. It was a wonderful experience, but I was curious as to what had transpired at Martin Luther King School. I later learned that one of the teachers from the lounge had told my CT I said the smell in her room was coming from her. What I didn't know was the smell really was coming from her because she had a medical issue. When I spoke to my supervisor about the issue, she explained that she and those in her department at the university felt the new report was contradictory since the initial report from my CT was written only a week earlier. They weren't convinced that anyone could receive such a glowing report one week and a contradictory one the next week, so they dismissed the unfavorable report. I was relieved.

A bright spot in my college experience came when some of my professors encouraged me to run for homecoming queen. I was twenty-four years old with two children and never thought I would win. But I accepted the challenge and mounted the stage, answering every question posed to me. One question set me aside from the rest and captured the judges' attention. We were all asked to expound on our definition of true beauty. I explained that true beauty had nothing to do with the kind of good looks one would use to describe Farah Fawcett Majors. It was not from luck or inheritance, but it had more to do with the kind of person you are, your character, and the way you treat people. That answer won me the crown. Against all odds, I became the university's first black homecoming queen in October 1978. Our football team won that night after a substantial losing streak, and I represented them on the field with my pale yellow gown, low-cut Afro, a tiara, and a borrowed fur stole from my friend, Barbara. It was a memorable night that made me proud.

The only other unfortunate incident I experienced during my college tenure was during my time as a work study student in the president's office. My job was to look through several news media for any articles or information referencing the university. The information was then glued into a scrapbook, along with previously posted information. But President Maxwell's secretary decided she wanted me to forgo my duties and, instead, assigned me the tasks of vacuuming the carpet in the office, cleaning the dishes, making coffee for the president's guests, and walking to the supermarket to shop for items to restock the office pantry. Those were not my duties, and I felt insulted that she would ask me to do them, especially since other work study students hadn't been asked to do tasks outside of the job description. I voiced my concern, resulting in a phone call from the president. He apologized for the situation and assured me it wouldn't happen again. I accepted his apology, thanked him, and asked to be transferred to a different site. The request was granted.

Off campus, I had another unfortunate experience. I needed a routine medical procedure. Having worked for Hudson County Family Planning, I knew several doctors, and one such doctor worked in conjunction with the previous job I held. It made sense to go to him for the procedure because he was well respected and came highly recommended by many of his patients. I, too, had worked for him. I made an appointment, and when the time came, I went to have the procedure done. When I arrived at his office, it was dark inside. I paid no attention to that because I knew my way around as a former employee. I went in and was glad I was the doctor's only patient; that way, I wouldn't have to wait around for long. I needed to get back home as soon as possible to relieve the babysitter.

I undressed, put the robe on as instructed, and climbed onto the table. Nervous, I thought good thoughts because I'd never experienced local anesthesia and had to psyche myself out to avoid being frightened. I hated needles.

The doctor spoke to me softly and smiled to ensure me there was nothing to be frightened of. He said the needle would feel like a slight stinging sensation, and he would also give me a procedural sedation to help me relax even more. That, along with the encouraging words I had heard about him helped calm me. I lay there, closed my eyes, said my prayers, and put my trust in God and the doctor.

I began feeling lightheaded and woozy. I wanted to grab my head, but my hands wouldn't cooperate. They wouldn't move. My legs were heavy like lead and they, too, wouldn't move. I never did go completely to sleep, which bothered me because I thought being awake and aware meant I would feel pain from the procedure, but I didn't feel much of the pain, only slight pressure.

After the doctor completed his work, he called my name and asked if I could hear him.

"Yes," I responded in slow motion.

"Can you feel this, too?" I felt his mouth and tongue on my vagina.

I felt myself flinch, and I tried to pull back from him. I pleaded, "Stop, please stop. Please don't do that. I want to leave."

God knows I tried to rise from the table, but I couldn't. I had neither the strength nor the frame of mind. He placed his tongue on my clitoris and began moving it swiftly until he forced me into multiple unsolicited orgasms. The anesthesia began to wear off. I was regaining movement of my arms, and I flung them wildly, trying to hit him and get him away from me, but I wasn't yet sober enough to make a connection or get close enough to him.

He stopped abruptly. His work was done, and I rolled over to help myself up. I fell off the table, and he didn't bother to help me up. He walked away like he was getting out of a taxi and crossing the street to get to his next destination. I pushed myself up and got dressed; I pulled my pants up but left them open because I was still under the influence of the sedation and didn't recognize that they should be closed. My blouse was open also. I ran, staggering from the building into the darkness that waited outside.

I walked toward my car in a zigzag motion. My strength was slowly returning, but I clearly couldn't operate an automobile. I was so frantic about what just happened that I still hadn't stopped to button my blouse or pants. Then I saw my friend Barbara's husband.

He grabbed me. "Hey, Phyllis, what's wrong with you, girl? Why are your clothes hanging off you like that? What happened to you, girl?"

I told him bits and pieces. It was enough for him to piece together what happened. He asked me where my car was. I was still dazed. I told him where I thought my car was, but I was mistaken. My sense of direction was off. He buttoned my blouse and closed my pants then walked with me until I located my car.

"You are in no shape to drive," he said. "Sit here for a minute. I'm going to get you some food so it'll absorb some of the grogginess and help you focus."

He returned with a fish sandwich. I took a bite but told him I had to go home to my children.

"Are you sure you can drive like this?" he asked.

It didn't much matter if I could or couldn't, I needed to get home to my children. "I'm fine," I said. "Thanks, Ernest." And I was off.

I sideswiped a few parked cars before I finally got out of the city and onto the highway. I swerved across Highway 280 until I arrived home. Once inside, I thanked the babysitter, then fell across my bed and slept for two hours before waking up to find her still there with the girls. She said I didn't look well, so she decided to stay until I woke up. Thank God she did.

I felt so confused when I awakened. I recalled the incident and could not understand how something like that could've happened. It seemed like a dream. I felt violated, dirty, abused, and angry. He was a powerful man, a well-respected, upstanding man in the community and state, a doctor known for his philanthropic gestures. I, on the other hand, was damaged goods in the eyes of our society. I had what they would consider a past. But as the days went by, I got angrier. I had no one to discuss it with; James surely wouldn't understand. I thought he would somehow find a way to make it my fault, as I had witnessed so many times growing up when women made accusations. Society always found a way to justify men's bad behavior. So I began asking hypothetical questions, and some people suggested I call the Department of Human Rights. I spoke with a Caucasian woman who, after learning who the doctor was, advised me to forget about the idea of pursuing anything to do with the incident—as if that's all it was, an incident. She had scared me more than helped. I was twenty-four and had no influence or status in life other than what I had made for myself, and I was naïve about these matters. She said anything I had ever done, any sexual encounters, and any legal violations, right down to a simple parking ticket, would be open to discussion. I wasn't concerned about those things and was willing to accept that. Then she said my children would be dragged into it, and things would get very ugly. With no money for an attorney and no family support, a single black mother of two children living in what many would perceive to be a slum area of an inner city, with only a high school education, I didn't stand a chance. Nor did I want to put my children at risk of any undue ridicule. They had done nothing. Her words haunted me. They echoed in my head repeatedly like a warped 45 with a bad needle. I felt even more wounded. So as misguided as it was, I went with her advice. I dropped the matter and endured the internal pain just like the other sexual assaults that dangled on to each piece of my heart.

I had to do something, but my inexperience hindered me. My only recourse was to make an anonymous phone call to his residence. When his wife answered, I told her what he had done.

She said, "Don't call here again with this nonsense. I will report you to the telephone company and have them file criminal charges against you!"

Although nothing beyond the call was ever done, I felt a small sense of vindication. I began a private investigation of my own, asking questions about him, and, to my surprise, I learned that I was, by far, not his only victim. It seemed, however, no one was willing to come forward, so every accusation was just conjecture. I thought if his wife had heard my words and any one of the other rumors circulating about his perverted behavior, maybe my phone call would at least give her pause to the possibility of truth. Whether it did or not, I'd never know. I never went back to his office again. In fact,

I never heard anything about him again, until years later when he passed away.

My remaining undergraduate experience went uneventful. And on a rainy day in May of 1979, my mom, sister, brother, and James witnessed me receive a bachelor's degree in elementary education with a minor in behavioral science. I had done it! I finished in just four and a half years, going two years in the evenings and two and a half years during the day. I attended all summer sessions and any interim sessions to make up for the credits I couldn't earn when attending full-time evenings. I had made good on my promise to Mrs. Davis, Mr. McGhee, and myself.

For the first time, I felt like adulting had its privileges. I had coveted one of the most significant accomplishments, and now, it was time to step into a different world. I needed to look for a job in my chosen profession. After taking the advice of my next-door neighbor's sister, I made a trip to the East Orange Board of Education to apply for a language arts position at a middle school. With no experience, I completed the paperwork and was directed to visit the Hart Complex, where I was interviewed by Ralph Milteer, the vice principal of the school. My inexperience led me to pay close attention to every detail of the interviewer. He asked questions about my background, and I noted that when I said I was from Suffolk, Virginia, he wrote a question mark on his paper behind the word "Suffolk." When the interview was over and he asked if I had any questions, my gut told me to expound on my place of birth and the name "Milteer," which I knew well. I had gone to school with several of Ralph's relatives who shared the name. And as we continued the conversation, it turned out that we were actually cousins. I knew the job was mine.

I was hired for my first teaching position in August of 1979. I proudly shared my new accomplishment with my welfare caseworker, so I could be removed from the welfare roll. He congratulated me and expressed how proud he was of my accomplishments. He added that my monthly stipend wouldn't end for another two months because of the way the system worked. I asked how to go about returning those funds because I didn't want to get caught up in welfare fraud. He explained that the funds wouldn't have to be returned and should be used to offset my monthly expenses, since new hires usually had to work at least two weeks before receiving a first paycheck. In my case, it was one month, so the checks were welcomed.

Samuel T. McGhee, director of admissions,
Jersey City State College (1975)

Phyllis, Jersey City State College homecoming queen (1978)

Phyllis, Jersy City State College graduate

CHAPTER 36

School Days

"D-Day" arrived! I had heard all the negativity about the school, including chaos and a lack of supervision. I knew there was a police officer on duty at all times. Stepping into the situation with no experience seemed like it would be a challenge. And I knew no one. I was on my own. I was nervous as I accepted my role, along with a teacher's grading pen (red on one end and blue on the other), a grade book, a plan book, a box of white chalk, an eraser, and a voluminous purple and white teacher's edition English grammar textbook. Everything was fine, except the textbook—it was intimidating. I had no experience, and the book read like a Greek tragedy, leaving me feeling like I was about to endure some form of suffering without the benefit of an accompanying catharsis. But I knew myself; I would press on. I would figure it out. I went home and cracked that book open, beginning with page one, leafing through each section with trepidation, excitement, and wonder. I made a personal vow that I would do what was necessary to see this thing through. I would do my best with every child who sat under my tutelage. I would find my way, and if a day came when I felt I might do more harm than good, I would have the good sense to leave the profession.

School started, and I was left to greet my very first class of twelve, thirteen, and fourteen-year-old eighth graders. The William S. Hart Educational Complex had an interesting structure. We referred to it as open classroom, an instructional technique with a great deal of supported philosophy behind it. The idea of the open classroom was to have a large number of students of varying skill levels housed in a single space, with several teachers present. The concept was a model of the one-room schoolhouse but often with more than two hundred students in a single multi-age, multi-grade classroom. The Hart Complex practiced a modification of the open classroom concept. In fact, it was more like the open-space concept, which was introduced to the United States in 1965 as an experiment at an elementary school in the South. At the Hart Complex, this concept included a large, high-ceilinged loft separated into two areas by one long wall but with no doors. Each of the two areas was designed to have four class areas because there were no actual rooms. The floors were carpeted to buffer the noise of the foot traffic, and each of the four class areas were without walls to separate the language arts, mathematics, science, and social studies class areas. However, as teachers, we followed the social conventions of teaching in traditional manners, as if the walls were still present. This meant movement was limited because the four core teachers claimed their open space by partitioning it with rolling chalk boards and file cabinets. This, of course, did nothing to muffle the sound of our voices as each of us delivered instruction. I found it to be a challenge but also an opportunity for growth. From my classroom, I was able to hear how my colleagues taught lessons and approached discipline. It helped me, since I had no experience from which to reference.

I was tried by fire, learning quickly how to manage a classroom.

The first test came when an all-out fight broke out on the other side of our loft. We could hear children stampeding the area, trying to get to the fight. However, when I listened even closer, I observed that the math, science, and social studies teachers on our side of the loft never budged. Their students didn't move, and instruction continued. I knew it was a defining moment for me. If my students moved and I did nothing, it would send the wrong message; I would become the weak link on our team. I braced myself and waited. A few students began to look antsy and started squirming in their seats like they were attempting to get up and go to the fight.

I am unsure of where my words came from, but without hesitation, I turned and looked them all in their faces and said, "If you dare move, I will break your legs."

After the words flipped off my tongue, I quickly realized I probably should have handled the situation differently, but before I could consider any other approach, those squirming, antsy students sat still and gave me a quick eye roll before coming back to order. I knew then that I was on to something great. I was establishing my classroom management style and these students were my test subjects and would share my style with the next year's group.

I later learned that was exactly how it was done. It is how a teacher's reputation begins to precede her. Therefore, I had to be careful to always send my intended message by saying what I meant and meaning what I said. There was no time for mixed messages, especially as a novice teacher.

I was catapulted back in time to the voices and styles of my own teachers. I remembered them well and found inspiration from them, even the teachers whom I felt could have used some guidance of their own. I recognized their lack of skill as an area to improve in my own practice.

As the years progressed, I realized that much of my practice was a version of several of the teachers who had left indelible marks on me: Mrs. Davis, Mrs. Blizzard, Mr. Downing, Mrs. Bennett, Mr. Copeland, Mrs. Fisher, and Mrs. Bembry.

Mrs. Davis and Mrs. Blizzard had shown me how to make concessions for marginalized students. Mr. Downing taught us the meaning of follow through when it came to completing homework assignments. Mrs. Bennett made sure we remained middle school students, not focused on growing up too quickly. Mr. Copeland unknowingly shaped the way I understood history. And by the time I reached high school, Mrs. Fisher pointed me in the right direction for books, while Mrs. Bembry taught me that I wasn't a bad math student; I had just encountered some bad experiences with some inexperienced teachers. These experiences, and so many more, shaped who I became as an educator. I was known for my compassion and understanding of my students. I became their support in a variety of ways when, many times, it seemed no one else cared to support them. And I loved them, even when they didn't love themselves or were lacking love in their homes. I went above and beyond the call of duty, as many of my colleagues did. I often highlighted the victim or underdog, taking him or her under my care for that year and beyond because they represented me at one time in my school experience. If they needed clothing to wear to the eighth-grade dinner dance, I purchased it. If they needed an outfit for the promotion exercise, I bought it. I even provided housing for some of them, allowing them to take up residence in my home.

I kept in touch with Mrs. Davis over the years, and she remembered me right up through our last conversation, when she was in her early 90s. In fact, she called me by my full name when I asked her if she knew who I was. "Yes," she said, "I know who you are. This is Phyllis Bivins. How are you? Did you ever become a teacher?"

Tears rushed forward, but I didn't let her know. Instead, I

responded, "Yes, Mrs. Davis, I did become a teacher. As a matter of fact, I became a very effective teacher because of you. I took everything I learned from you and incorporated it into my practice, so I would address the whole child, not just the academics."

She was happy to learn that I had become a teacher, not just any teacher, but a Mrs. Mary Alice Davis teacher. I attribute my overall success as a teacher to Mrs. Davis. My state of poverty urged her to take action, and that action taught me what it meant to be a teacher, meeting the needs of the whole child in a diverse population of children who come with a variety of needs, which is what Mrs. Davis encountered when she met me. I was thankful that she'd had such an influence on my life. She taught me to bloom wherever I was planted. I guess I had a profound impact on her practice as well.

Phyllis's first class as a teacher, William S. Hart Middle School (1979-1980)

Phyllis, graduate school, Oxford University (1992)

Graduate school graduation day: (L to R) Daughter Tawana, Phyllis, Daughter Zammeah, and goddaughter, Shavonne (1993)

CHAPTER 37

Another Ending with a New Beginning

Christmas 1980 was a high time for the girls, my sister, my mother, James, and me. Mom had come from Jersey City to East Orange to spend the holidays in our home. This was a first, and we were excited and determined to shower her with love, kindnesses, kisses, hugs, and gifts. Then at about three a.m., I received a phone call informing me that the building on Bayview Avenue, where Mom lived, was on fire. She lost everything. By His grace, she had us, so Mom was now a permanent fixture in our home. We all doted on her and she learned to love it.

By August 1981, my mom encouraged me to allow her to take the girls with her on vacation to visit her youngest sister, Ida, who had moved back to Virginia. I was elated. It was Mom's forty-seventh birthday, and she wanted to spend it with her sister and granddaughters. A day or so after her birthday celebration, I received a phone call from my older daughter, Tawana, who was eleven. She was frantic.

She said, "Mom, Granny, is throwing up in the bathroom sink, and it's all blood!"

Being so far away, I didn't know what else to do but have her call Ida. Ida immediately called for an ambulance. Mom was hospitalized. She spent the next few days in ICU after a surgical procedure, which resulted in a lobectomy. Mom was a heavy smoker and drinker, and she was diagnosed with tuberculosis. Just six days after her forty-seventh birthday and before I could say goodbye, she passed away. My heart never experienced such pain and grief. I was sad and lonely. I felt a void that would never be filled because no one could have loved me more than my mother. I have never loved anyone so intensely, outside of my children.

Despite my incredible loss, I returned to my classroom in September a different person, with a different kind of responsibility. I was now my sister's guardian. I had to care for Tawana, who was entering grade six, Zammeah, entering grade two, and Annette, who was out of school but deciding what to do with her life. I recommended college. She enrolled into Kean University but left after two semesters and enlisted into the United States Navy.

I returned to John L. Costley Middle School, and my return was met with condolences, cards, a fruit basket, and colleagues trying to cheer me up. My teaching assignment was a different experience, too. It was the only time I was allowed to loop, where I remained with the same group of students for more than one year. We stayed together for three years. During our time together, I was able to do good work with them by addressing not just academics, but all their needs. I became what every teacher is at some point in her career—teacher, confidant, parent, spiritual advisor, friend (to an extent), social worker, counselor, disciplinarian, and so much more. To establish a familial atmosphere in and outside of our classroom, I even had a sleepover one weekend for all the girls. The boys were jealous, of course, and wanted to do the same thing; however, instead, I treated all of them to lunch at a local establishment. Years later, one of the girls, who now practices law, called me just to say hello. She reminded me of that weekend sleepover and said she never forgot how it made her feel. Our conversation reminded me of something I'd once heard the late Maya Angelou say: "People will forget what you say, but they will never forget how you made them feel." I was always concerned with how I made my students feel because I remembered how my teachers made me feel, without me having to wear my woes on my sleeve.

I had a successful career as a middle school teacher of both urban and suburban children. Several parents over the years told me I had become a household name, which always positioned me in good standing with them.

I thought transitioning from urban education to suburban would be a challenging adjustment. What I learned is that children are children. The major difference between the urban and suburban children I taught was economics. The question I had was whether I would experience the same kind of reception from suburbia I had garnered in the urban setting. That question would be answered soon after I accepted my second teaching position in the town in which I live, South Orange.

Minutes before I signed the contract for my new position, I received a phone call advising me that I would need emergency surgery. In a state of panic, I immediately shared the information with HR, who assured me there would be no problem. I didn't begin my new job in September as planned but in late October instead. My eighth graders waited patiently to meet their new teacher. I knew no one and felt like the new kid on the block. But one student, Susan Flores, sensed my newness to the school and staff. She took me under her wing and showed me the ropes as I would have done with any new student. She advised me as to which staff people to avoid, which parents would be difficult to deal with, how to acquire what I needed from the office staff, and which students required special attention. She was incredible.

In January of the same school year, I received another call from my doctor, informing me that I would, again, need surgery. I was out of school for another eight weeks. Concerned about the amount of time I had missed as a first-year teacher in a new school district, I began stressing about how I would catch up, how I would make up for the sixteen weeks, and how I was being perceived by the parents of my students. Three days after my surgery, one of the nurses came in and helped me into a wheelchair, telling me she was taking me to a private waiting room on the hospital floor near my assigned room. Puzzled, I went along. When I arrived in the large waiting room, thirty students or more and several parents stood, armed with balloons, gifts, cheers, laughter, and a basket full of goodies that included a poetry book by my favorite poet, Maya Angelou, home-made cookies, chocolates, and other treats. It was overwhelming but such a lovely expression of love and genuine concern. I had a difficult time fighting back the tears, but I knew I had impacted their lives from the time I arrived in October until the end of December, just before I was hospitalized in January. God had shown me favor. He had given me magic, and I had the "it" factor, as we often said about teachers who were considered natural educators.

While there, I earned a master's degree in English literature, a supervision certification and a principal's license. Equipped with all the required credentials, I left suburbia and headed back to urban education in another local urban city, Paterson. This time, I arrived as a member of the administrative team.

I wore several hats in my new position. I was a coach, facilitator, HIB (harassment, intimidation, and bullying) coordinator, lunch supervisor, vice principal, teacher, testing coordinator, director of the after-school tutorial program, coordinator for National Junior Honor Society, building disciplinarian, coordinator of the black history program, mentor, and more. With the exception of coach and facilitator, I handled the positions simultaneously. I learned to juggle my time and organize my day in such a way that no responsibility went lacking. While the tasks were daunting, I used the opportunities to continue to grow, develop, and help students. The small, less than 400-student public school ranged from kindergarten through grade eight. And there were plenty of opportunities to practice my craft. I learned that I was good at reaching children of all ages. I was also good at reaching their parents and providing them advice that would benefit their sometimes misguided children. I received many verbal and written accolades from students and parents expressing their gratitude for the work I had done with their children.

My approach to children, parents, and teachers remained a direct correlation to my childhood and the teachers who provided the guidance I needed to become a successful student and teacher.

Finally, as a student, I achieved the ultimate—a doctorate degree in education leadership. The countless hours I'd spent with my dissertation, juggling two jobs, and engaging with family was an arduous enterprise well worth the effort. The entire year leading up to August 2007 was intoxicating and intense. Excitement filled every space in my circle of family and friends as we prepared for Miami, where I would be conferred, Dr. Phyllis Geneva Bivins-Hudson. I had lived for this day for the past four years, and now it was within my grasp.

Family and friends arrived in Florida, settled into our hotel, and waited. My exuberance spilled over, making the moment exciting for everyone. That morning, we all rose earlier than needed, prepared for the short trip to the graduation site with time to meander before the fanfare. I was bursting with energy, but I couldn't help feeling that Murphy's Law might be lurking. Would my name be forgotten? Would an error be discovered? Did I still need to fulfill a requirement? Had I neglected a payment? The questions floated through my mind like wavelengths. However, I looked to the sky where I knew God was listening and acknowledged that He had shown me favor. I had become my family's matriarch and their rock. I was there, in that place, still raising the bar for my children. I would return home feeling worthy of the work and time devoted to this important accomplishment that would finally satisfy my insatiable appetite for education. My internal motivation and validation had been sated. I only wished Mom could have been there to share this incredible moment.

Now, as a retired teacher, I spend my time in schools mentoring principals and in classrooms mentoring new teachers and sharing with them some of the experiences that made me culturally competent and successful in my own classrooms. I talk about how I interacted effectively with my students because of the way my teachers interacted with me. They ensured my needs were met by addressing the whole child. I teach novice teachers to question their practice and their thinking about children. I challenge them to look to the other side of their own lives and breath the air of their students for more than a moment to help them realize that, while they may have good intentions, they have to be deliberate about seriously addressing the needs of all students and meeting each of them where they are, with the understanding that where they are might not be where they think. I support them by guiding and coaching them, helping them to develop their own competence and understanding. I discuss with them ways to implement theories but also how theories go out the window when they meet children who are like I used to be. We look at alternative strategies because my teachers recognized my physical needs and addressed them before addressing my academic needs. Finally, I challenge them to look deeply inside themselves and reflect on why they want to teach. And when they do, I suggest they make decisions about their practice, the children they serve, and the commitment they must make to each child, so every child in their charge has a chance at success, now and in the future. I wouldn't trade my journey for anything. Although I endured a great deal of pain, I pushed through it, and I survived. I have learned, and I have decided to bravely and boldly stand before classroom teachers and students whenever and wherever possible to tell my story because I realize, by doing so, I may be saving someone else.

Phyllis, doctorate program graduation, Nova Southeastern University (2007)

CHAPTER 38

Final Thoughts: Mom, Family & Education

Thoughts of my past still carry the aroma of poverty, abuse, and the fractured relationship I had with my mother, but my spirit of dedication, strength to overcome seemingly unsurmountable obstacles, triumph over tragedy, self-reliance, courage to share my story, and, ultimately, forgiving my mom is what brought me through this journey.

Maturation came with a price; however, every endurance of pain, stress, disappointment, and happiness propelled me into the success I have achieved along the way. I have had nothing short of a stellar career doing what I love. I have been an educator for more than forty years. Although I am retired, I am not tired; therefore, I continue to do what I love through education consulting and training teachers. In fact, it was with teachers where I created a platform to share my story. In doing so, some were uncomfortable; however, their discomfort did not impact my courage to take back my victimization. I learned that talking through my story was my way of processing it. While in earlier years I could not get through it without tears, constant interaction with it has given me triumph over tragedy. It allowed me to see who I really am—a strong woman who was able to overcome obstacles that may have rendered others helpless or led them to engage in destructive behaviors. Thoughts of my past still resonate with me, but I am whole despite it all.

In my travels, both locally and abroad, I find myself reaching out to those who seem less fortunate than me. I have brought people into my home for that reason. There have been times when I have given too much, even to the point where I have gone without. But it makes me feel good. I relish in those moments when love bends the air and I can make life just a little sweeter for someone else, even if it's just for a moment.

My past also taught me to be watchful of my children. Their sleepovers were held at home. I never felt comfortable leaving them at a home with a man present. I had learned that, too many times, girls fell victim to unsolicited sexual advances or some kind of secret perversion. I wasn't willing to risk it. And the relationship I longed to have but lacked with my mom made me a better mother. I have stayed connected to my children's lives and made them feel loved and cared for from the cradle. I ensured they had stability in their lives. Being transient was a thing of the past. We relocated only to improve our status in life. Education was a focal point from the time they were babies. We always talked about it, and even though I struggled through the girls' early school years, they never knew it. They attended the best private schools, including a prestigious all-girl high school for Tawana and a boarding school for Zammeah, where she was the recipient of a full academic high school scholarship. They both went on to great colleges—Hampton and Howard University—and became productive citizens, with rewarding careers. One day, when someone asked them when they knew they were going to college, they both looked at each other and said, "We never thought we wouldn't go to college. It just seemed like an extension of high school." And that's the way I wanted it to be. They are good wives, wonderful mothers, and active members of our sorority, Delta Sigma Theta Sorority, Inc., where we proudly serve our community together.

Along the way, I met my husband, Curtis, an unbelievably wonderful man, and from that relationship, I gained an amazing son, Eric, who was only four years old when we became mother and son. As an adult, he is a well-established A-list record producer, musician, and song writer, with an impressive discography. He knew from as young as four years old that he wasn't interested in a college career, but wanted a successful career in music, following the footsteps of his father.

As for Mom, I recognize that she did her best to make sure every stopover in every town where she'd left me in someone else's charge yielded a precious gem, worthy of note, because they were the ones who helped fill a void that Mom knew she couldn't. I continue to respect and pay homage to my mother because of her unacknowledged worth and the love she exuded toward me. I will be forever indebted to her for the temporal comfort she afforded me when life clearly could have been so much worse. Mom had a woman's dignity and a mother's love for her children, and in her resolve, I believe she knew that out of all the darkness that befell us, a brighter dawn would light our way. I think she relied on me to make that happen. She had instilled in me a determination, and on my own, I learned that there is power in a strong will. Every beating she endured, every sacrifice she made in the name of her children, positioned me to be closer to her and gave me a renewed courage to rebuff the hard times that rolled over us in seemingly endless bouts of sheer terror and uncertainty.

I know now what I was incapable of understanding while I was living my experiences. Although my life did not amount to milk and honey, I had to experience each dreadful moment in preparation for my future. I chose to see a break in the clouds rather than become a victim of circumstances. And my teachers played a serendipitous role by inadvertently training me as a child to become the educator I would eventually be. Each lesson they taught, whether academic or moral, about relationships or reasoning, compassion or patience, helped shape some of the qualities and characteristics I harvested over the years to develop my craft and practice. I was identified as a master teacher. I was selected as Teacher of the Year. I was a mentor to some of my colleagues. I've been commissioned to write programs for teachers and train novice teachers. I've written curriculum and consulted with administrators, supporting their role in ensuring educational strategies are in place that support effective learning. I chose to push through the poverty-stricken conditions in which I was born to gain respect and create a productive life for myself and my family. I recognize that every step of my journey was intentional. I understand that had I not experienced this life in the exact way it unfolded, I would not be the person I am today. For me, this has been a pilgrimage, and my sacred place has been the institutions of learning of which I've been privileged to be a part. But those institutions were not always schoolhouses. I have learned much about people, but more importantly, I have learned about myself. I've gained an understanding of who I have become and why I am compelled to engage in the ways that I do. The biggest revelation of all is that writing this book forced me to speak my truth out loud and recognize that I am who I am because my mother and father were who they were.

Because of Mom, I am a healthy, active, and vibrant woman. My husband, Curtis, and I have been happily married for the past twenty-five years and together for twenty-nine. He has been my rock and my supporter throughout our fairytale relationship, a father who's always been present for our three children, and a doting grandfather to our four granddaughters. I have been blessed beyond measure. Life is grand!

FAMILY PHOTOS

(clockwise): daughter Tawana, Phyllis, daughter Zammeah (2015)

Phyllis (2015)

Phyllis and husband, Curtis (2017)

Phyllis and son, Eric (2018)

Third oldest granddaughter, Kai Ishara (2020)

Oldest granddaughter, Kamili Amani (2020)

Second oldest granddaughter, Kafi Khikhiua Maati (2020)

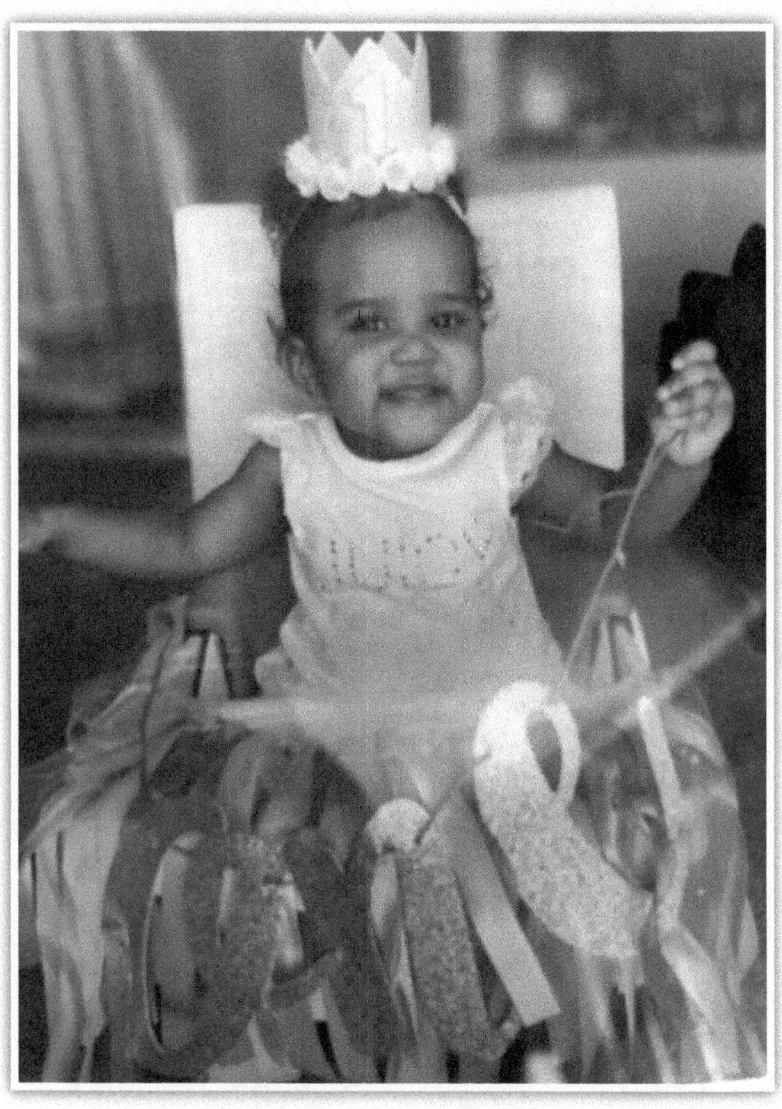

Youngest granddaughter, Nyla Lee (2020)

(L to R): daughter Tawana, Phyllis, daughter Zammeah, members of Delta Sigma Theta Sorority, Inc. (2019)

ACKNOWLEDGEMENTS

This book would not be possible were it not for Geneva Smith-Bivins, my dear mother. Although she left us only six days after turning forty-seven years old back in 1981, I still remember the genuinely sweet and caring person she was. I am sad that she is not here to see this finished product, but I know if she is somewhere looking, I feel certain I have her approval. Thank you, Mom. I am sorry you will never know the impact you had on my life. Your every trial and tribulation made me a stronger woman and a better mother. I miss you.

To my first born, Tawana Latrice Bivins Rosenbaum, after Mom, you were the second in line to make this work possible. You are between every line. Because of you, I became a mother. Because of you, I was forced to live a life worth living to ensure your well-being, your stability, and your education. You have always been one of my biggest cheerleaders for all my projects. And you were my first inspiration for writing way back when you were a mere fifth grader. I love you so much and feel so blessed to have been given the opportunity to be your mom.

To my second born, Zammeah Monique Bivins-Gibson, because of you I became a better mother. By the time you arrived, I had three and a half years of experience. So, thank you for that. Thank you, also, for the inspiration to write this book. It has truly been a labor of love. You know exactly when it began back in 2003, when we sat together, forced to be still. You encouraged me to pen the first draft during that time together. I love you very much and deem it a blessing and a privilege to call you daughter.

To my son, Eric Lee Hudson, thank you for your encouragement. You made me want to get this thing right because you always demonstrated respect for my credentials and my abilities that I sometimes take for granted. When I shared my story with you when you were but a boy, I thought you were not listening, but I learned through the years you were indeed listening, evidenced by your constant reminders of how proud you are of me, considering my humble beginnings. Thank you for believing in me. I love you to pieces, and I'm proud to call you my son.

To my favorite oldest granddaughter, Kamili Amani Rosenbaum, thank you for all the moments we have shared as BFF's talking about my childhood and how to connect the dots so it could be shared with our family in a way that would memorialize it and bring to your attention just how important education is. Thank you for being a different kind of confidant and believing in me, even when there were times when I just wanted to move on to something different. I love you to the moon and back.

To my favorite middle granddaughter, Kafi Khikhiua Maati Rosenbaum, thank you for allowing me into your world. I know how guarded you can be, but with me, you have always been a source of inspiration. My childhood, unlike yours, lacked stability; however, I see so much of your character in me—your love for writing, your exceptional penmanship, your sensitivity, your attention to detail, the quality of your work, and the fact that you are an overachiever. I love you more than you will ever know.

To my favorite third granddaughter, Kai Ishara Gibson, you will never know the internal excitement I experienced when you sat and listened with such intensity while I read an excerpt to you from my book. Your words after my reading will never depart from me. You said, "Wow, MeMa, that's so interesting. I can't wait to read your book." Thank you for that, Kai. It was a source of unexpected inspiration, but truly well-accepted. I left you that day with a renewed spirit and a willingness to continue writing. I love you fiercely.

To my husband, Curtis Lee Hudson, thank you so much for the many nights and days of reading and re-reading my manuscript. Thank you for answering the litany of questions I constantly had, and thank you for encouraging me, even when I was trying to encourage you to write your own book. Most of all, thank you for being a great critic with a keener eye than you think. You are also an incredible listener, offering sound advice and suggestions in places I hadn't even considered. I love you from the bottom of my heart.

To my dear, sweet sister, Cynthia Annette Bivins-Alston, thank you for allowing me to dote on you as a child the way I did. I loved you like you were my very own, and as we have both acknowledged, sometimes we thought you were mine because I was often your primary caretaker. Thank you for the conversations we've shared remembering 421 Roy Street and the craziness that went on there. I love you, girl. You are my bestie and absolutely the funniest sister in the world.

To my uncle, Willie Thomas Smith Sr., thank you for your contribution to this work. I enjoyed talking with you and reminiscing about the old neighborhood and those wonderful weekends with you down on S. Lloyd Street in Suffolk. You provided an important piece of knowledge to help fill in some of the missing spaces. And thank you for always coming to visit me—visit *us*—back in Suffolk on Roy Street. You can't begin to know the relief I felt just having you around. I love you, Unc.

To my uncle Benjamin Franklin Smith, thank you for always

believing in me and encouraging me to be the best I can be. Thank you for those visits to Roy Street back in Suffolk when Pam and I were little girls, listening to every word you had to share. I will always remember those crazy joy rides leaving the cops in the dust. And those weird sandwiches you used to make. You provided some much-needed relief when I was going through some tough times. I love you for that and so much more. What an awesome and funny uncle you are.

To my brother-in-law, Wade Hudson, you will never know how excited I was when you agreed to be the first reader of my first draft of this work. You—a very accomplished and prolific writer in your own right—provided me with some much-appreciated feedback and constant encouragement. Whenever we saw each other at family events or other events, we always found time to talk about your work but also my progress, even if just a little bit. Thank you for the encouragement and for not giving up on me. I love you, brother-in-law.

To my friend, confidant, soror, and boss, Heather Harris-Ngoma, thank you for your encouragement. I have never met anyone so encouraging as you. You have been with me on this journey since the first time I mentioned my intentions. You have prodded, questioned, and suggested a variety of ways to help me make this thing happen. Well, it has happened, and I am eternally grateful to you for your role in it. You've shared some of your own writing, sent me to places where I could improve mine and so much more. I love you, soror.

Many times, throughout this project, I was forced to use generic words to describe places, streets, etc. because I had forgotten them over the years. I would be remiss if I did not thank you, my oldest friend, Barbara Jean Harris. You became my researcher and fact checker. Your memory is incredible. Thank you for the late-night texts and phone calls forcing you to dig deeply into the crates of your memory for information that happened between 1962 and 1970 when I left Virginia. Because of you, my words are richer. I love you, friend.

To all my elementary and high school teachers who may still be with us, thank you for the village of contributions you invested in me. To you, Mrs. Susie Bennett, with whom I am in touch via FB, thank you for developing in me a sense of urgency to get what you were imparting. Thank you, also, for caring enough about me to be a parent to me when you needed to, by making me aware that I was a seventh grader and had ample time to grow up. I have that and other fond memories of you. Thank you for that and so much more.

Tim McGhee was a gentleman and friend I will never forget. I will always be reminded that through his generosity and compassion I was able to walk through a door of hope when he made it possible for me to begin my college career at, then, Jersey City State College. I am eternally grateful for that. I am only saddened by the fact that Tim passed away a few days before I submitted my book, while I was in the middle of writing this acknowledgment to him. I intended to share a personal copy with him.

When I learned that I needed an editor, I didn't know where to start. Then I read *Trust Issues*, which happens to have been written by my cousin. I inquired about who assisted her with self-publishing—Monique D. Mensah. And the rest is history. I can't thank you enough for your caring and patient approach to the novice writer. I had the ideas but didn't know what to do beyond that. You led me to the finish line. Thank you for your professionalism and making this seem easy, when, clearly, it isn't. I don't know what I would have done without our conferences, emails, and phone calls.

Thank you for reading *Flying on Broken Wings*
If you enjoyed this book, please help spread
the word by leaving an online review.

KEEP IN TOUCH WITH PHYLLIS

Website: www.genceptz.com
Facebook: Phyllis Bivins-Hudson
Instagram: @dr.pgbh
Twitter: @pgbhudson

Made in USA - North Chelmsford, MA
1181315_9780578744094
02.10.2022 0950